David Philip Lindsley

A short course in business shorthand

David Philip Lindsley

A short course in business shorthand

ISBN/EAN: 9783337215439

Printed in Europe, USA, Canada, Australia, Japan

Cover: Foto ©Andreas Hilbeck / pixelio.de

More available books at **www.hansebooks.com**

A SHORT COURSE

IN

BUSINESS SHORTHAND

FOR THE USE OF

Amanuenses, Clerks, Secretaries, Professional and Business Men.

ALSO ADAPTED TO THE USE OF STUDENTS

IN

HIGH SCHOOLS, ACADEMIES, COLLEGES, AND SEMINARIES.

BY

DAVID PHILIP LINDSLEY.

AUTHOR OF TAKIGRAFY.

CHICAGO:
D. KIMBALL, 85 Madison St.

BOSTON:
OTIS CLAPP & SON, 10 Park Place.
1888.

PREFACE.

This is not a first book; though, if the student wishes to begin in the middle of the subject and work both ways, this is just the book he will want to commence with. To aid him as much as possible in this course, should he prefer it, an introductory chapter is given which epitomizes the author's treatment of the Simple Style. Still he does not recommend the student to trust to this epitome; he should learn the Simple Style from some of the complete works on that style; such as the Elements or Exercise Book.

THE STYLE TAUGHT IN THIS WORK.

Between the territory occupied by the Simple Style and that occupied by the Reporting Style there is a wide field, and one just now most hopeful. It is believed that at least nine-tenths of our students of shorthand need, and desire, an intermediate or business style, in which a fair rate of speed can be secured with the least loss of time in learning, and with the greatest degree of legibility and accuracy.

To provide just such a style has been the object of the author from the first. The easy reporting style written twenty-five years ago, and used in manuscript. was written with this design. The Note-taker published in 1872 aimed to solve the same problem; but the author was carried beyond his original intention by the great desire of many persons to master a reporting style. This stenographic pressure led to the publication, in 1882, of the HAND BOOK, which satisfied the demands of the reporting style, but left the great middle style entirely unrepresented.

Four years ago the author prepared a series of manuscripts for teaching a Business Style which he has used in his private classes ever since. But for various reasons their publication has been postponed until the present time. It seems almost unaccountable that the publication of the style which the author has always regarded as of "the greatest use to so large a number," should have been delayed so long. There are, however, doubtless, some compensating advantages in the delay. Something must have been learned through the extended experimentation of the past years. Doubtless the style here represented is the more perfect for the delay, and the manner of presenting it, it is hoped, has also been improved.

The style here represented is adapted to the wants of at least nine-tenths of all professional writers of shorthand in the country. The court reporter is necessary, but only a limited number of places are open for this work. Thousands of literary and professional men need a still easier style, but will not cultivate it. Nearly all Amanuenses need just this style, and thousands of students who are pursuing courses of higher education also need it. With so wide a field to fill, it must not be supposed that all who use it will stop at the same point of development, but this is not necessary. This work will put all on the road to the speediest and surest success.

The author takes pleasure in offering this little work to the teachers of shorthand writing, as the best expression of his method of teaching yet made. The work is so arranged as to be adapted to any plan of instruction which the teacher may choose; and as every exercise has its accompanying key, it can be used by the pupil without a teacher better than any previous work.

Assured that its use will greatly facilitate the study and practice of the art, the author sends with it his heartiest greetings, begging the friends of other days to give it a kindly reception and candid criticism, and to continue to co-operate with him in introducing the advantages of the art to the millions who are waiting to receive it at our hands.

THE AUTHOR.

Philadelphia, Pa., October 1st, 1888.

CONTENTS OF TYPE PAGES.

Introduction—Application of the terms System and Style—
Natural Styles, ... 9
Actual Styles, . . . 9
Two Theories of Teaching, ... 10
A Knowledge of the Simple Style Useful to Amanuenses, 11
Method of Study, ... 12, 13
Length of Courses of Study—New Principles, . . 14, 15

CHAPTER I.
REVIEW OF THE SIMPLE STYLE.

Section 1. Alphabetical Drills—Par. 1, Consonants; Par. 2, Vocals; Par. 3, Compounds of the El, Ar and Qua Series; Par. 4, Compounds of the Circle Series, . . . 17
Section 2. The Joining of Vocal and Consonant Signs 19
Section 3. Primary Long Vocals, ... 19
Section 4. Secondary Long Vocals, . . 21
Section 5. Short Vocal Joinings, ... 23
Section 6. Short Intermediate Vocal Joinings, . . 23, 25
Section 7. Long Intermediate Vocal Joinings, . . 25
Section 8. Explanations of the Qua and Triphthong Series, 25
Section 9. Key to Table of Word and Phrase Signs, . . 27
First Test Exercise, ... 27, 31
Second Test Exercise, . . . 31
Third Test Exercise, . . . 33, 35

CHAPTER II.
GENERAL CONTRACTIONS.

Section 1. Additional Word- and Phrase-Signs, 37
Writing Exercise 1, ... 37
Section 2. A tick for final y, initial h, and shortened I, 39
Section 3. The Use of Vowels in Words of one syllable, 39

CONTENTS.

Writing Exercise 2. Vocalized Outlines, . . . 41
Writing Exercise 3. The Child and the Brook, . 41, 43
Writing Exercise 4. Selections for Practice, . . . 43, 45
Writing Exercise 5. Selections for Practice, . . 45
Section 4. Words of a Single Stem containing Signs of the El, Ar, Qua and Circle series, . . . 45
Section 5. Extended use of the Compounds of the El and Ar series, ... 45
Section 6. The use of Zhe for j and nj, . . . 45
Section 7. The use of the Circle where the Vocal is included, 47
Writing Exercise 6, Illustrations of Sections 4, 5, 6 and 7, and additional phrase-signs, ... 47
Writing Exercise 7. Selections for Practice, . . 49
Writing Exercise 8, " " . 49
Section 8. Shortened Letters, . . . 51
Writing Exercise 9. Shortened Letters, . 51
Writing Exercise 10. Selections for Practice, 53
Section 9. Lengthened Curves, . . 55
Writing Exercise 11. Lengthened Curves, . 57
Section 10. Miscellaneous Contractions, . . . 59
Writing Exercise 12. Selections for Practice, . 59
Section 11. Ste and Est Loops, . . . 61
Writing Exercise 13. The n and v-hooks, the shaded Em, El, Ar and Ra, Ste and Est loops, . . . 61, 63
Writing Exercise 14. Selections for Practice, 63
Writing Exercise 15. Application of Principles, 65
Writing Exercise 16. Selections for Practice, . 65, 67

CHAPTER III.

SYLLABLE SIGNS—PREFIXES AND AFFIXES

Section 1. Extended use of the Half-Length Principle, ate, way, ment, etc., ... 69
Writing Exercise 1. The Terminations ate, ward, dent, ment, etc, ... 69
Writing Exercise 2. Selections for Practice, 71
Writing Exercise 3. Selections for Practice, . 73
Section 2. The Terminations zhn, shn, zhnal, shnal, 73
Section 3. The Terminations meter, liter, ure, ural, urally, ual, ually, ular, ularly, tude, ize, ness, less and with, . 75

CONTENTS, 7

Section 4. The Terminations ian, ien, iar, ier, ior, with
i coalescent, ... 75
Section 5. The Terminations ed and ing, . 75
Writing Exercise 4. Affix Signs, . . 75
Writing Exercise 5. Selections for Practice, . 77
Writing Exercise 6. Selections for Practice, . . 77
Section 6. Contracted Prefix Signs, . . 79
Writing Exercise 7. Prefixes, . . 81
Writing Exercise 8. Selections for Practice, 81
Writing Exercise 9. The Discovery of America, . 83
Section 7. Contracted Phrases and Word Omissions, . 85
Section 8. Punctuation in Note Taking, . . . 85
Writing Exercise 10. Special Phrases, . 85, 87
Writing Exercise 11. Selections for Practice, . 89
Writing Exercise 12. Selections for Practice. . . 89
Writing Exercise 13. Extract from a Lecture by Edward
Everett. The Temperance Reform, . . 91, 93, 95

CONTENTS OF ENGRAVED PAGES.

CHAPTER I.

Alphabet: 1—Consonant, 2—Vocals, 3—Compounds of the El,
Ar, and Qua series, 4—Compounds of the Circle Series. 16
Joinings of Vocal and Consonant Signs, Primary Long
Vocals, Secondary Long Vocals, . . . 18, 20
Short Vocal Joinings, ... 22
Short Intermediate Vocal Joinings, . . . 22, 34
Long Intermediate Vocal Joinings, . . . 26
Consonant Joinings: A, with Angles; B, without Angles; C,
Miscellaneous, ... 28
Table of Word- and Phrase-Signs, . . . 28
First Test Exercise, . . 30
Second Test Exercise, . . 32
Third Test Exercise, . . . 33

CHAPTER II.

Writing Exercise 1. Additional Word and Phrase Signs, . 36
Writing Exercise 2. Vocalized Outlines, . . 38
Writing Exercise 3. Selections for Practice, . . 40
Writing Exercise 4. Selections for Practice, . . 42

8 CONTENTS.

Writing Exercise 5. Selections for Practice, . . 44
Writing Exercise 6. 1 and 2 Vocalized Compounds, 3 Vocals included in Compounds, 4 Zhe used for j and nj, 5 Zhel used for jel,and Zher for jr. 6 Vocals included with Circle, 7 Additional Phrase Signs, ... 46
Writing Exercise 7. Selections for Practice, . 48
Writing Exercise 8. Selections for Practice, . . 50
Writing Exercise 9. Shortened Letters. . . . 52
Writing Exercise 10. Selections for Practice, . . 54
Writing Exercise 11. Lengthened Curves, 56
Writing Exercise 12. Selections for Practice. . . 58
Writing Exercise 13. The n- and v-hooks, Emp, Arch, Arj, Ler, Rel, Ste and Est, ... 60
Writing Exercise 14. Selections for Practice, . . 62
Writing Exercise 15. Miscellaneous Outlines in application of the General Principles of Contraction, . . . 64
Writing Exercise 16. Selections for Practice, . . 66

CHAPTER III.

Writing Exercise 1. The terminations of ate, ward, bent, dent, vent, ance, ins, ... 68
Writing Exercise 2. Selections for Practice, . 70
Writing Exercise 3. Selections for Practice, . . 72
Writing Exercise 4. The Terminations ation, ition, asion, ision, ection, ution, tional, vation, ulation, ure, ual, ular, ship, self, tude, ize, ization, ian, ien and with, . . 74
Writing Exercise 5. Selections for Practice, . . 76
Writing Exercise 6. The North American Indians—Sprague, 78
Writing Exercise 7. Contracted Prefixes ad, com, con, intra, tre, tri, tro, trance, intrance, extra, tre-tri, expli, em, im and pro, ... 80
Writing Exercise 8. Selections for Practice, . 82
Writing Exercise 9. Discovery of America—Everett, . 84
Writing Exercise 10. Word Omissions, Intersections and Special Phrases, ... 86
Writing Exercise 11. Selections for Practice, 88
Writing Exercise 12. Selections for Practice, . . 90
Writing Exercise 13. The Temperance Reform—Edward Everett, ... 92-94

INTRODUCTION.

APPLICATION OF THE TERMS SYSTEM AND STYLE.

The terms, system and style as applied to Shorthand, are sometimes used interchangeably. In this work a 'system" of Shorthand Writing is regarded as comprising all the various styles, modes or degrees of contraction, built upon a given alphabet by a given author.

The word "Style" relates, not to the complete work of an author, but to any one form or variation of it which may be adapted to any specific purpose.

In the system of Takigrafy we recognize two classes of styles one natural and necessary, the other subject to such modifications as convenience may dictate in adapting it to use.

NATURAL STYLES.

A natural style is a natural development of a system upon a given alphabetic basis.

The first natural style which may be called the LITERAL consists of the joinings of the alphabetic letters into word-forms without modification, change or variation. Such a style may be of service in teaching children, but is not in actual use.

The second natural style is built on the basis of the alphabet as supplemented by the compounds of the Qua, El Ar and Es series. This, with little variation, forms what is known as the Simple Style.

The third natural style is based on a further extension of the alphabetic basis, formed by the addition of shortened and lengthened letters, final hooks, prefix and affix signs, etc. This style may admit of a greater or less number of fundamental stem signs. In Phonography the stem signs number not far from 1500. In the Contracted Style of Takigrafy the most extended alphabetic basis is reduced to about 500 stem signs; though this number is by no means fixed, as it can be lessened or increased, according to the degree of contraction required, and the object for which the style is cultivated.

ACTUAL STYLES.

The styles in actual use are based upon the natural styles, but admit of some variation, in the use of a greater or less number of word- and phrase-signs.

THE SIMPLE STYLE.

The Simple Style, as used, has for its basis the alphabet supplemented by the signs of the Qua, El, Ar and Es series; and every legitimate outgrowth of this basis belongs to it. But whether the Word-signs it employs shall number 25, 50 or 100, is purely a matter of convenience, and their use or disuse does not affect the character of the style. So in regard to the use of Phrase-signs; whether they shall be used at all, or if used, under what restrictions, are open questions that do not affect the validity of the style.

The style used in this work which may be termed the Intermediate, Amanuensis, or Business Style, is built on the same natural basis as the third "Natural Style" described above; and differs from a full Reporting style, not so much in the contractions which form its basis, as in the manner of their use. The use of half length letters is admitted, but their use is restricted principally to their phonetic value, as expressing the union of the sounds without an intervening vowel. The use of lengthened curves is also admitted, but their use is restricted. So this style does not differ radically from the Reporting Style, but is a rudimentary, and less difficult form of that style; or one in which the contractions are used in their phonetic value. This makes their application as natural and easy as the use of the Compound Signs in the Simple Style. The few irregular outlines can be easily mastered, and one having a perfect knowledge of the Simple Style can master the Business Style in a few weeks.

In the author's conception of the art, the Simple Style is necessary to the Contracted. The Simple Style embodies all general principles, while the Contracted Style deals with special principles. The Simple Style is an essential part of the Contracted, and its principles enter into the outlines of thousands of words even in the briefest style. It is a great mistake to suppose that in a Contracted style all words are contracted, or that the study of contractions can ever be made to take the place of a study of the general principles which form an essential part of all the Styles of the art.

THEORIES OF TEACHING.

To those unacquainted with the subject, it may be necessary to say, that two theories of teaching have grown up. One theory of late vigorously pushed assumes that the chief difficulty in learning the art is in gaining the habit of using certain word-forms without hesitation, and that this is to be acquired, not through a knowledge of principles, but through practice on them. To reduce this labor to a minimum, it aims to teach the briefest form for each word at its first introduction to the student. This presents the art to his mind as a system of word-signs, or stenographs. It is substantially the old stenographic method of teaching, which has prevailed from time immemorial. It has, of course, some points of merit; for, to a certain extent, word-signs are necessary, and those in frequent use may well be learned in an early part of the course.

IN BUSINESS SHORTHAND. 11

ADVANTAGES OF THIS METHOD OF TEACHING.

The advantages claimed for this plan are:
1. That it is easier to teach a pupil to write a stenograph than to tell him why it is so written; that the faculty of imitation is more widely diffused among men, than the ability to comprehend principles.
2. That the teacher saves time spent in experimentation by the other method, and need not be troubled with the correction of exercises.
3. That the student in imitating a perfect copy, is saved the trouble of blundering, as he is likely to do if he attempts to apply a principle instead of copying a word form.

OBJECTIONS TO THIS PLAN.

The objections to this plan of teaching are:
1. That it lays no foundation for a complete knowledge of the system.
2. Beginning nowhere it ends nowhere. All that the student acquires is a stenograph for a certain number of words. Unusual words, and the universe of proper names of persons and places, are so many stones of stumbling, as they can be properly handled only through a knowledge of principles.
3. It destroys the essential principles of Takigrafy, in destroying the Simple Style.
4. It arrests the true development of the art turning it backwards towards its stenographic sources.
5. It starts the student on a course of study without method, with the certainty that if he ever acquires any reasonable knowledge of principles, it will be after years of practice, and a great loss of time and effort. What the teacher gains the pupil loses by this plan of work.

The teacher may indeed shirk his duty, but a certain amount of experimentation on the part of the pupil is essential to any knowledge of principles, and the Stenographic method of teaching does not remove but simply postpones the difficulty. This will be seen when we consider that only a very small part of the world of words can ever be taught in a course of instruction, and if they could be taught they could not be retained in the memory.

A KNOWLEDGE OF THE SIMPLE STYLE USEFUL TO AMANUENSES.

The value of c knowledge of the Simple Style to amanuenses and reporters, as well as other writers, is in the fact, that by far the greater number of words in the language must be written in that style. The contractions apply to a limited class of words; while the almost endless number of words of infrequent occurence must be written through a knowledge of the principles alone, not through any previous knowledge of the Word Forms.

The theory of teaching which the author has followed, and which he believes to be the only theory through which certain and speedy results can be obtained, is to teach first those principles which apply to all words, and to accustom the pupil to write from a knowledge of the principles of the art, until he has a command of the system as taught in the Simple Style. This lays a broad foundation for future requirements, upon which he can build a style more or less contracted according to the work which he proposes to do. Upon this foundation he can erect his superstructure, and it will stand; and having acquired what contractions, word- and phrase-signs he needs, his knowledge is complete, harmonious and intellegible. Should he at any time desire, he can add other contractions; or should he find, through change of business, that he does not need the briefer style, he falls easily back upon the broad foundation of the Simple Style, and the art remains to him a sure possession for life; whereas the stenographic plan of study above described, leaves him with a style which he cannot adapt to new circumstances; and his acquirements are lost; and like other stenographers he goes back to longhand writing.

This is not mere theory. The author has taught hundreds of pupils according to both methods. He has carefully noted results through a series of years, and frequently pupils who have insisted on being taught in a stenographic method have confessed in after years that they were convinced of their error and that they had lost time instead of gaining it; but he cannot recall one instance, in which a pupil has regretted having learned thoroughly, and practiced fully the Simple Style.

Should any student or teacher inquire how much time should be devoted to the Simple Style, I would say: The more the better. If the student is so situated that he can spend one or two years in the practice of the Simple Style, it will be greatly to his advantage. In cases where this cannot be done, where the student is anxious to acquire the art for immediate use in amanuensis work, he should spend at least two months on the Simple Style; even if but one month remains for the study of contractions.

METHOD OF STUDY.

The student should first ascertain whether he is prepared to go on with the following work: Have you mastered the principles of the Simple Style? Have you reduced them to practice so as to write easily, at least, seventy-five to eighty words a minute, and in a tolerably correct manner? If you fall far short of this in speed, or are not able to apply the principles of the style to the formation of good outlines, you can do nothing to lead to a rapid and permanent success so well as to go back to the Exercise Book or the Manual, and practice the principles of that style.

To test the students ability and to give at the same time a review of the Simple Style three test Exercises are given accompanied by

Keys,* with the speed in which they should be written, indicated. Should the student fail on the first trial, let him proceed to master the word-signs of the Simple Style as given in Chapter 1, and with this additional knowledge try his speed on these exercises once more. If he still falls short in speed but is confident that he is correct in his knowledge of the principles of the Simple Style, let him take up the alphabet drill and persevere in it day by day until he can write the entire alphabet, vowels and consonants, in ten seconds. He will also in connection with this practice take up the consonant joinings as given on pages 19 to 25, devoting fifteen to twenty minutes or more every day to the exercise. He should attend especially to the joinings of the short vocals and the table of consonant joinings given on page 28. Vocal joinings should be written as read by some one employed to dictate them; but the consonant joinings can be repeated, writing the same outline as many times as possible in a minute or half a minute at a time.

It will be found that such joinings as Be-Te, Te-Be, can be written a hundred and twenty-five to a hundred and fifty times in a minute, and such combinations as Ish-La, Ish-En, Ma-Ith, etc., in which no angle occurs, two hundred times and upward in a minute. This kind of practice should be continued for weeks devoting a short time each day to the excercise.

These drills may accompany the study of the Student's style, when the student is prepared to enter upon it. His lack of speed will in many cases be found to be owing to his previous neglect of these and the alphabet drills, and nothing more may be necessary to enable him to reach the test proposed above.

STUDY OF THE BUSINESS STYLE.

After the student has passed the test, and has been duly admitted into the study of the style given in this work, he should proceed in the order of the exercises laid down, determined to carry each point with him as he proceeds; for he has now reached a point in which theory must yield to practice. Avoid the slovenly habit of a mixed style in which the word and phrase signs of the simple style are used with variations. This may be well enough for the teacher whose business it is to go back continually to elementary principles, but not for the student who wishes to gain speed. Use the forms given in the tables always and everywhere; and when a

*In case the student has learned forms of contraction not used in the Simple Style. this test of speed should be made in the style to which he is accustomed. It would not be advisable for him to endeavor to conform his style to the forms given in the engraved Key in such a case.

new form is learned bring it into practice and use it. Go no farther, nor faster than you can go in this way. By following this plan you will gain in speed and ability with each succeding chapter.

If, after spending a week or two on these drills, and on a review of such features of the Simple style as may require it, the student still finds himself unable to reach the speed indicated, there must be some difficulty either in his manner of working, or in his knowledge of the style which should be sought out and remedied.

TWO METHODS OF STUDY.

Having entered upon the study of the Business style in Chapter II, two courses lie open to the teacher and pupil; he can write the exercises from the type key without any previous study of the engraving, and then compare his work with the engraved page; or he can first study the engraving, and copy it preparatory to writing it from dictation. In either case, he can make his knowledge of the exercise practical only by drilling on it. After the word forms have been learned, so that he can write them correctly and readily, he should have the exercises read to him several times over, until he can reach the speed mentioned at the bottom of the exercise. Those exercises in which no speed is marked should also be written, not however with reference to speed, but with special reference to correctness of outline. Every other exercise in Chapter II, and every third exercise in Chapter III, are of this character, and are designed to teach the principles of the art through examples. The remaining exercises are designed to teach pupils to apply the principles in writing.

Where the length of the course admits of it, it will be well to pause after every half dozen lessons and write other exercises of suitable character, as a further test of the knowledge of the principles studied. How much time should be spent in this way will depend upon the amount of time which the pupil can command for the study.

LENGTH OF COURSES OF STUDY.

This leads to the observation that the courses of instruction in our shorthand schools are too short. The teacher who attempts to teach the art in three months time, must omit many things that should be taught. While it remains true that Takigrafy is vastly simpler than the old phonography and can be taught in much less time, still we should avoid the superficiality common among phonographers. They have filled the country with incompetent stenographers through the imperfections of their styles, and their method of training. We owe it to ourselves, to our pupils and to the art, to set them an example of more thorough preparation. We have done something in this direction, but not enough. Our courses of study should be extended from three and four to five and six months. The student can well afford to spend an extra month or two on his preparatory course, as it will result in most cases, in increased salary, and more permanent success.

Pupils sometimes come back for a second course after two or three years practice of the art, and in every instance, so far as I have observed, take, from that time, a higher position with enlarged remuneration. Let our competing schools aim at surpassing each other, not in the *shortness*, but in the *thoroughness* of their courses; or if some pupils are forced, by want of means, to realize on small investments in instruction, let them follow a partial course with the express understanding that the art is still beyond them, and that they have still much to do to make themselves masters of it.

NEW PRINCIPLES.

The new Alphabet as given in the Exercise Book is used in this work. It will be seen that the changes made are not so great as to hinder its use by those who have commenced with the older works.

The treatment of the prefix signs for *com* and *con* is the only change in general principles introduced, but the student will find many new forms of words and phrases which have come into use since the publication of the older works. A few phrases have been taken from The Amanuensis, compiled by Mr. Kimball, for which the author would make suitable acknowledgements; but he has not endeavored to copy the outlines taught in that work, or in the Hand Book, however desirable for the sake of uniformity such a course might have been, A uniform system of outlines is doubtless important, but it is not so important as it is that the art should be free to grow untrammeled, putting forth its branches freely, to be trimmed into beauty and harmony at a later period; when time and larger experience shall demonstrate the comparative value of the various forms thus introduced.

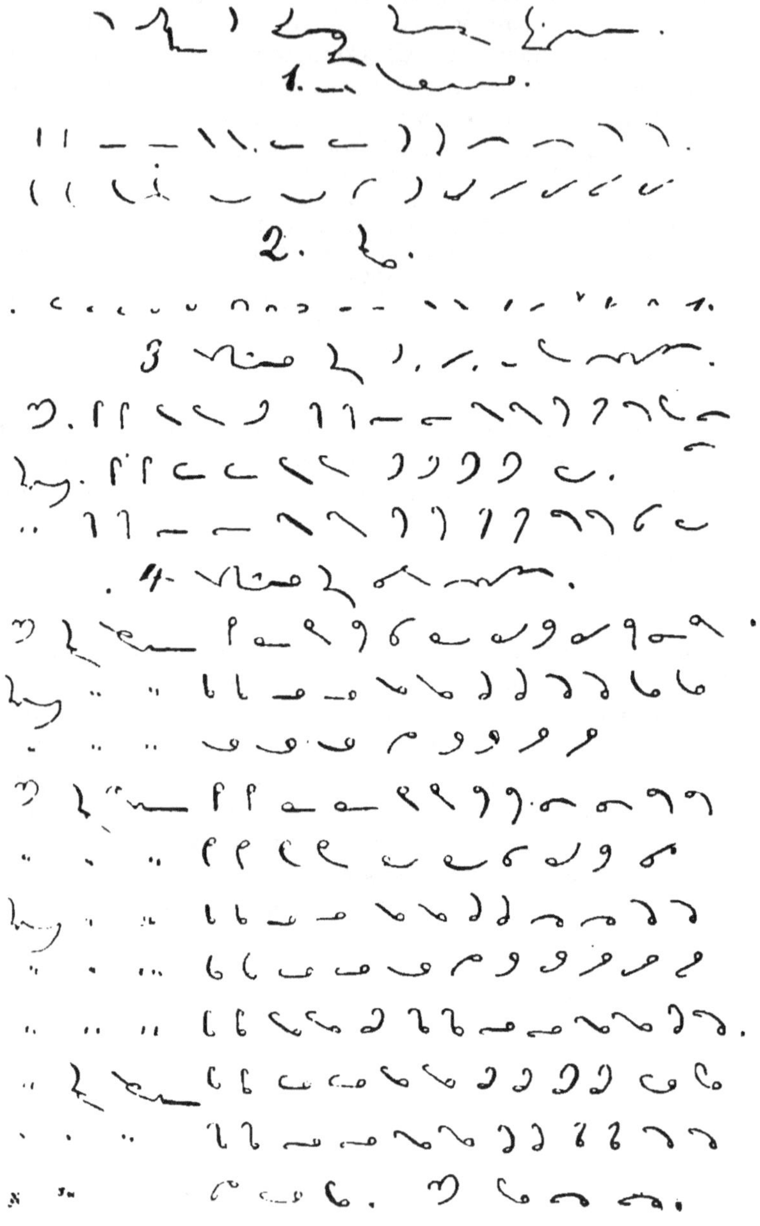

A SHORT COURSE IN BUSINESS SHORTHAND.

CHAPTER 1.
REVIEW OF THE SIMPLE STYLE.
DRILLS FOR SPEED.

1, Alphabet Drill; 2, Vocal Joinings; 3, Consonant Joinings. These Drills should be made to occupy twenty minutes every working day, or about one-twentieth of the time devoted to the art.

Speed attainable. On the alphabet—The entire alphabet in ten seconds, or less. The initial and final compounds (Sec. 3), in seventeen seconds. The signs given in Section 4, in one minute.

This page contains the entire alphabetic basis of the simple style, with many of the compounds repeated. Excluding repetitions, there are only one hundred compound signs, which, added to the forty-four letters, make only one hundred and forty-four signs as the alphabetic basis of this style.

THE ALPHABET OF LINDSLEY'S PHONETIC SHORTHAND.
(See engraving on opposite page.)

SEC. 1.—ALPAHBETICAL DRILLS.

I—CONSONANTS.

B P D T GA K J CHA V F Z S THE *ITH* ZHE ISH THA *ATH* N ING M L YA R WA HA WHA.

II—VOCALS.

A AI a at AH; E et it; OO oot; Out; AU ot; I OI EW OU.

III—COMPOUNDS OF THE EL, AR, AND QUA SERIES.

Initial: Bla pla gla kla fla. Bra pra dra tra gra kra fra shra *thra* qua dwa twa.

Final: Bul pul dul tul gul kul vul ful zhul shul nul. Ber per der ter ger ker ver fer zher sher ther *ther* mer ner.

IV—COMPOUNDS OF THE CIRCLE SERIES.

Initial, vocal excluded: Spe ste ske sfe sme sne sla sle swa. Spre stre skre.

Final, vocal excluded: Ebs eps eds ets egs eks evs efs eths *eths* aths *aths* ence enz engs ems else els ers erz.

Initial, vocal included: Sub sup sud sut sug suk suv suf suz sus suth *suth* suzh sush suth *suth* sun sung sum sul sul sur.

Final, vocal included: Bus pus dus tus gus kus vus fus zus sus thus *thus* zhus shus jus chus nus mus lus yus rus wus hus.

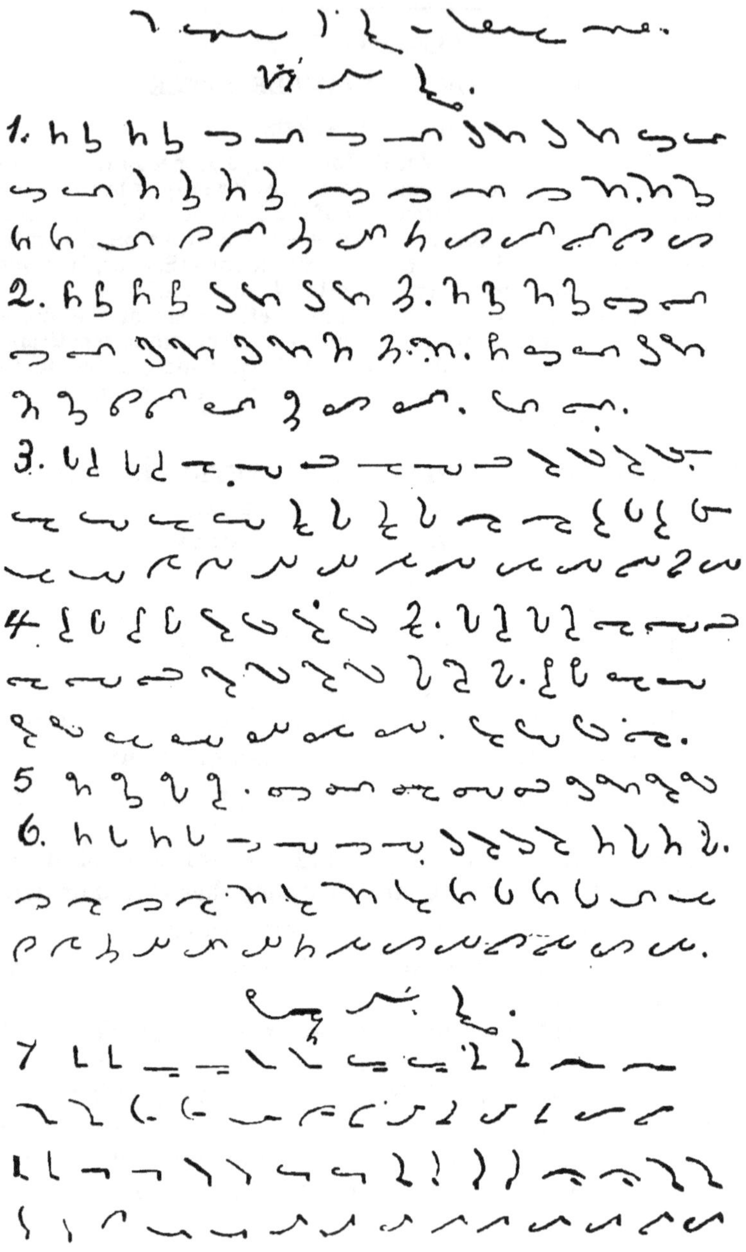

IN BUSINESS SHORTHAND. 19

Final, vocal included: Blus plus glus klus flus. Brus prus drus trus grus krus frus *thrus.*

Final, vocal excluded: Buls puls duls tuls guls kuls vuls fuls zhuls shuls nuls quuls.

Bers pers ders ters gers kers vers fers zhers shers thers *thers* mers ners quers.

Initial, vocal included: Ques, dwes, twes.

SEC. 2.—THE JOININGS OF VOCAL AND CONSONANTAL SIGNS.

In the table of joinings given on the preceding page, the variations of the vocal signs are given as nearly as possible in the order of the frequency of their occurence. It will be understood that the form of the vocal is determined by the convenience of joining with the letter that follows, as well as the letter that precedes it.

The tables wil serve a double use; as models of accuracy, and drills for speed. The student should first copy them with care from the engraved page, and then write them as dictated from the typic part by the reader. Repeat the drill until the tables can be written with accuracy and rapidity.

SEC. 3. PRIMARY LONG VOCALS.

(Key to the opposite page.)

Be be. Pe pe. De de. Te te. Ge ge. Ke ke. Je je. Che che. Ve ve. Fe fe. Ze ze. Se se. The *the the.* Zhe. she. Ne. Me me. Le. Ye. Re. We we. He he. Whe.

2. Ble ble. Ple ple. Gle gle. Kle kle. ˙Fle. Bre bre. Pre pre. Dre dre. Tre tre. Gre gre. Kre kre. Fre. Shre. *Thre.* Spe. Ste ste. Ske ske. Sfe sfe. Sme sme. Sne. Sle. Swe swe. Que. Twe.

3. Ba ba. Pa pa. Da aa da. Ta ta ta. Ga ga.⸳Ka Kate. Ja ja. Cha cha. Va va. Fa fa. Za. Sa. Zha zha. Sha shade. Na na. Ma ma. La. Ya. Ra ra. Wa wa. Ha ha. Wha.

4. Bla bla. Pla pla. Gla gla. Kla kla. Fla. Bra bra. Pra pra. Dra dra dra. Tra tra tra. Gra gra. Kra kra. Fra. *Thra.* Shra, Spa spa. Sta sta. Ska ska. Sna sna. Sla. Swa swa. Qua qua qua. Twa.

5. Spre spre. Spra spra. Stre stre. Stra stra stra. Skre skre. Skra skra.

6. Be ba. Pe pa. De da. Te ta. Ge ga. Ke ka. Ve va. Fe fa. Ze za. Se sa. The tha. *The tha.* Zhe zha. She Sha. Ne na. Me ma. Le la. Ye ya. Re ra. We wa. He ha. Whe wha.

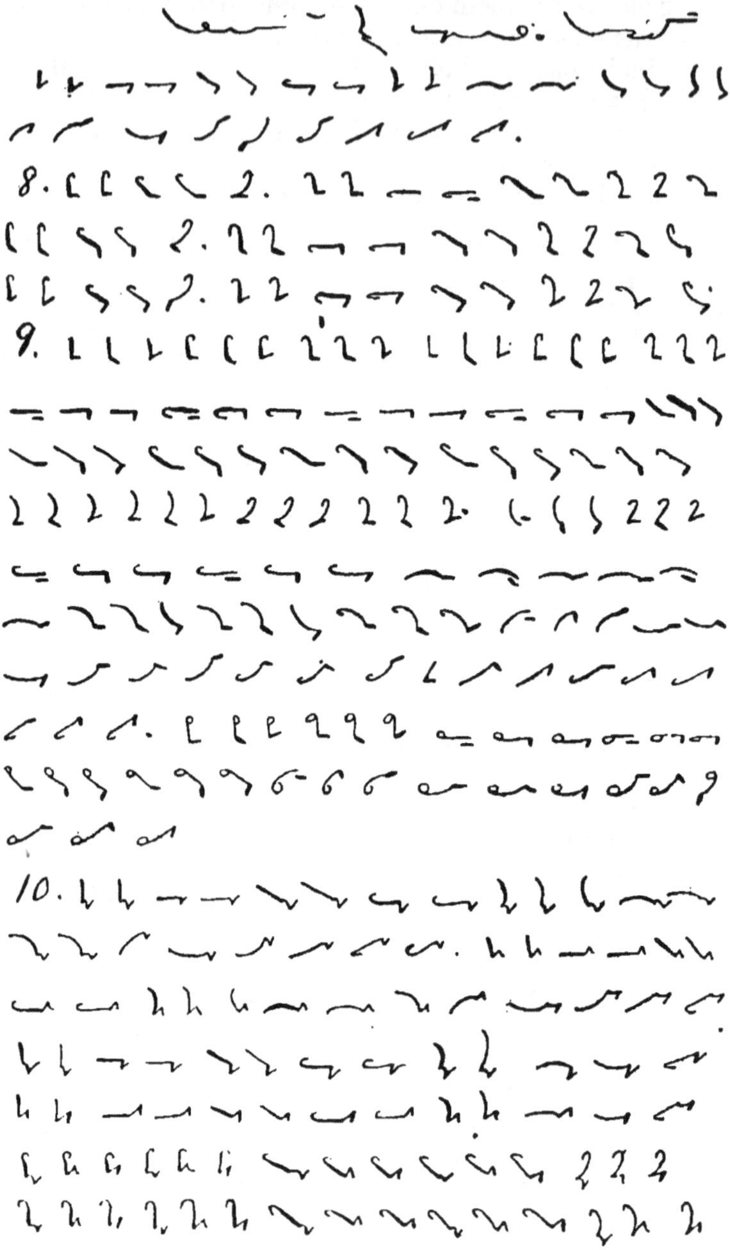

IN BUSINESS SHORTHAND. 21

Sec. 4.—Secondary Long Vocals.

7. Boo poo doo too goo koo joo choo voo foo zoo soo thoo *thoo* zhoo shoo noo moo moo loo loo yoo roo woo hoo. Bo po to do go ko jo cho vo fo vo fo zo so tho *tho* zho sho mo no no lo lo yo ro ro wo wo ho who. Bau pau dau tau gau kau jau chau vau fau zau sau thau *thau* zhau shau mau mau nau lau lau yau rau wau hau.

8. Bloo, ploo, gloo, kloo floo. Broo, proo droo troo groo kroo froo shroo *throo*. Blo plo glo klo flo. Bro pro dro tro gro kro fro shro *thro* quo. Blau plau glau klau flau. Brau prau drau trau grau krau frau shrau *thrau* quau.

9. Boo bo bau. Bloo blo blau. Broo bro brau. Poo po pau. Ploo plo plau. Proo pro prau. Doo do dau. Droo dro drau. Too to tau. Troo tro trau. Goo go gau. Koo ko kau. Gloo glo glau. Groo gro grau. Cloo clo clau. Croo cro crau. Voo vo vau. Foo fo fau. Floo flo flau. Froo fro frau. Shoo sho shau. Shroo shro shrau. Joo jo jau. Choo cho chau. Zoo zo zau. Soo so sau. Thoo tho thau. *Thoo tho thau. Throo thro thrau.* Moo mo mau. Noo no nau. Loo lo lau. Yoo yo yau. Roo ro rau. Woo wo wau. Hoo ho hau. Spoo spo spau. Sproo spro sprau. Stoo sto stau. Stroo stro strau. Skoo sko skau. Skroo skro skrau. Smoo smo smau. Snoo sno snau. Sloo slo slau. Swoo swo swau.

10. By py dy ty gy ky jy chy vy fy shy zy sy thy *thy* my ny ly ry hy why. Bew pew dew tew gew kew jew chew vew few shew zew sew thew mew new lew rew hew. Boi poi doi toi goi koi joy choi voi foi soi noi hoi. Bow pow dow tow gow cow jow chow vow fow sow now how. Bly blew blou. Ply plew plou. Gli glew glou. Kli klew klou. Fly flew flou. Bry brew brou. Pry prew prou. Gry grew grou. Cry crew crou. Fry frew frou.

Rem. It has not been the custom of the author to spend as much time in drilling on the long-vocal joinings as on the short ones, but they should not be wholly neglected. The great burden of work, in these drills, should be put on the alphabet page, and on the short-vocal joinings. Still the teacher should see that the pupil can write all the combinations given with perfect facility. A word cannot be written rapidly until the syllables of which it is composed can be so written; and great care has been taken in selecting the combinations, given in the preceding exercises, to give only those which actually form some part of an English word.

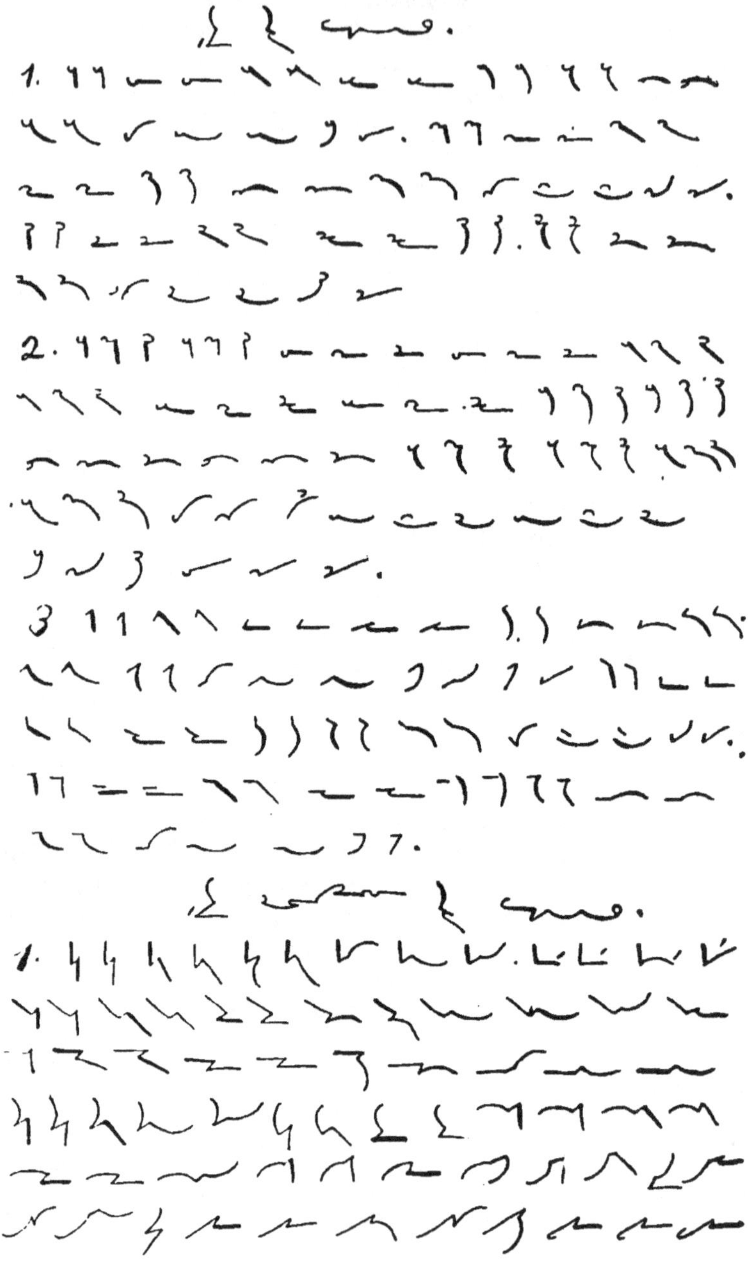

IN BUSINESS SHORTHAND.

Sec. 5.—Short Vocal Joinings.

1. Ab ap ad at ag ak aj ach av af azh ash az as ath *ath* am an ang al ar. Eb ep ed et eg ek ej ech ev ef ez es eth *eth* em en eng el er. Ib ip id it ig ik ij ich iv if izh ish iz is ith *ith* im in ing il ir.

2. Ab eb ib. Ap ep ip. Ad ed id. At et it. Ag eg ig. Ak ek ik. Aj ej ij. Ach ech ich. Av ev iv. Af ef if. Az ez iz. As es is. Azh ezh izh. Ash esh ish. Ath eth ith. *Ath eth ith.* Am em im. An en in. Ang eng ing. Al el il. Ar er ir.

3. Ob op og ok od ot oj och ov of oz os oth *oth* oth *oth* ozh osh om on ong ol ol or or. Ub up ud ut ug uk uj uch uv uf uzh ush uth *uth* um un ung ul ur. Oob oop ood oot oog ook ooj ooch oov oof oozh oosh ooz oos ooth *ooth* oom oon oong ool oor.

Sec. 6.—Short Intermediate Vocal Joinings.

1. Bob pop bog pock bosh both bomb bon bol bod pot boss bor gob cop cog cock cod cot coz goth con cong col koj top dock tog dot tot dof toss tom ton dong fob fop fog fon fol shop shock shod shot sob sop sog sock sod sot sol mob mop mod mol lop lock lot lodge lom lon lor rod rot roth rom rol hod hot wad.

2. Bab bib bat bet bit back beck pick baf bif bash bish path pith pam pem pim pan pen pin pal pel pil par per pir tap tip tat tit tack tick taf tif dash dish das des dis tas tes tis dath deth dith dam dem dim dan den din tan ten tin dal del dil tal tel til dar der dir tar ter tir bear pear dare tare gare care fair share their mare ne'er ware hair rare:

3. Gap gip cap kip gat git cat kit gag gig gaf gif caf gash cash gas guess kiss Gath geth kith gam gem gim cam kem kim gan gen gin can ken kin gal gel gil cal kel kil car ger. Chap chip chat chit Jack chick chaff jam jem Jim Jan. jen jin.

4. Fab fib fad fid fed fag fig fash fish fam fem fan fen fin fal fel fil far fir shab shap shad shat shag shack shav shaf sham shan shib ship shiv shif sheb shep shed shet shev shef shem shel sher sip sit sick sif sis sith sim sin sir sil map mip mat mit mag mig mif mish math mith man min mal mil mar mir nap nat nack naf nash nas nath nam nan nal nar lap lip lat lit lack lick laf lif las lis lath lash lith lam

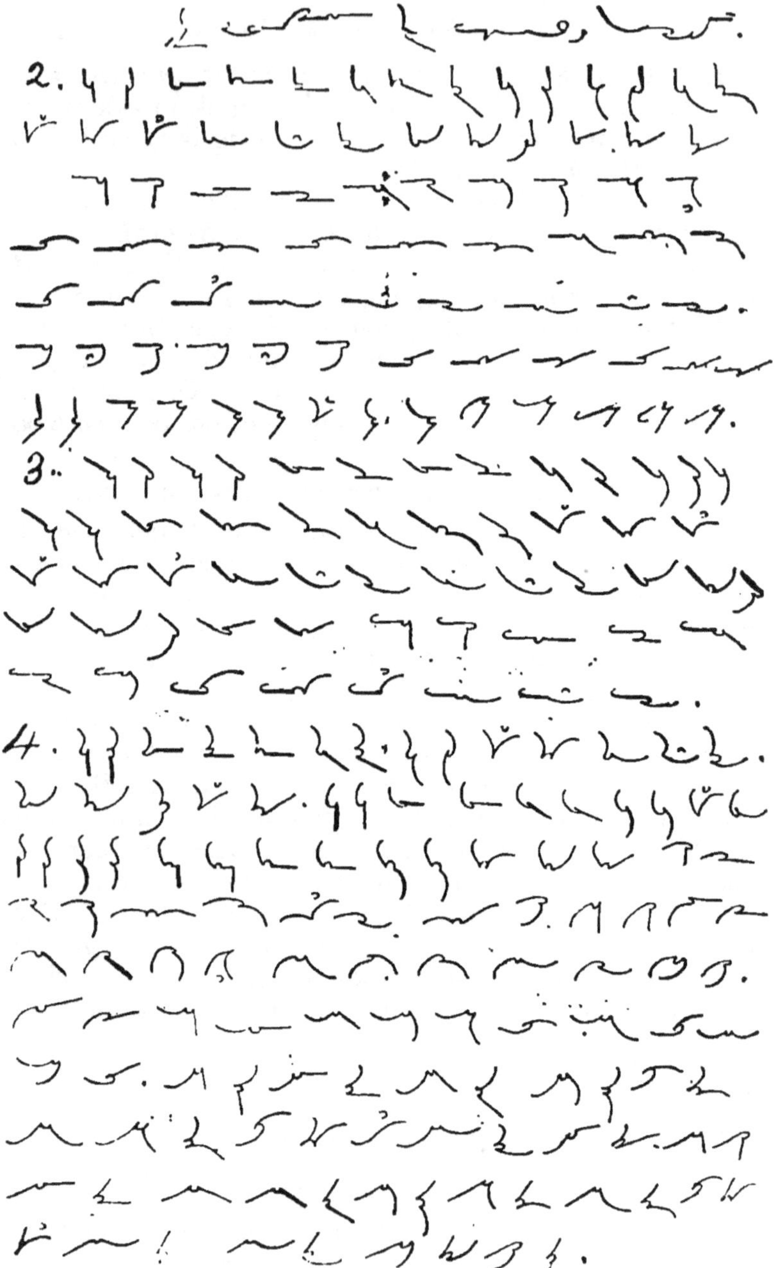

lem lim lan lin lar lir rap rip rat rit rack rag rig raf rif rash ris rath rith ram rem rim ran rin rang ring ral rel ril ril.

SEC. 7.—LONG INTERMEDIATE, VOCAL JOININGS.

1. Peep peak beat beef peace breathe bean beam peal peer. Deep teak deed tease teethe deem dean deal dear. Keep Greek keyed geese cream green keel gear. Phebe freak feed fees fleece feel. Sheep shiek sheet sheaf sheath sheen sheer fear. seek seat receive seethe seem seen seal seer thief theme. Meet meek mean meal mere. Need knees near neal.

2. Leap lead league leaf lease lean leal lear. Reap reek read reef wreath ream reel rear. Weep weed weak weave wheeze wean weal. Heap heed heave heath heal hear.

3. Babe bade bake page pave pain pail. Tape take date stave days dame Dane dale. Cape gate cake cage cave came Cain gale. Vague vain veil. Shape shade shake shave shame shale sake safe same sane sail. Mate make maize maim main mail. Nail nape snake nave naze name nation. Labor lade lake lave lays lathe lame lane. Rape rate rake rave raise rain rail. Yale hail wail hate Hague weight.

4. Boost booth boom boon pool poor poach post poet poem pore pawn pall. Toad dote dove dose tome tole tore taught talk tall. Coop goose cool. Gawk caught cause gall gone. Fool soup loop loom loon. Vote four foal shoat shoal shore mote more note knoll load lore wrote roach rove rose roar moth naught wroth wrought laud.

SEC. 8.—EXPLANATION OF THE QUA AND TRIPHTHONG SERIES.

1. The triphthongs, *spr scr str*, are written with special signs, as given in the alphabet page. When these signs occur medially and are followed by a stroke in the same direction, the hook need not appear. In other cases the hook shud be seen. In some cases the long sign is preferable.

2. The Wa or Qua signs, explained in the Exercise Book, are also given on the alphabet page.

Examples of the use of the signs will be found in the tables of joinings and in the test exercises which follow.

The consonant joinings on page 28 need no Key, but we add here a Key to page 29.

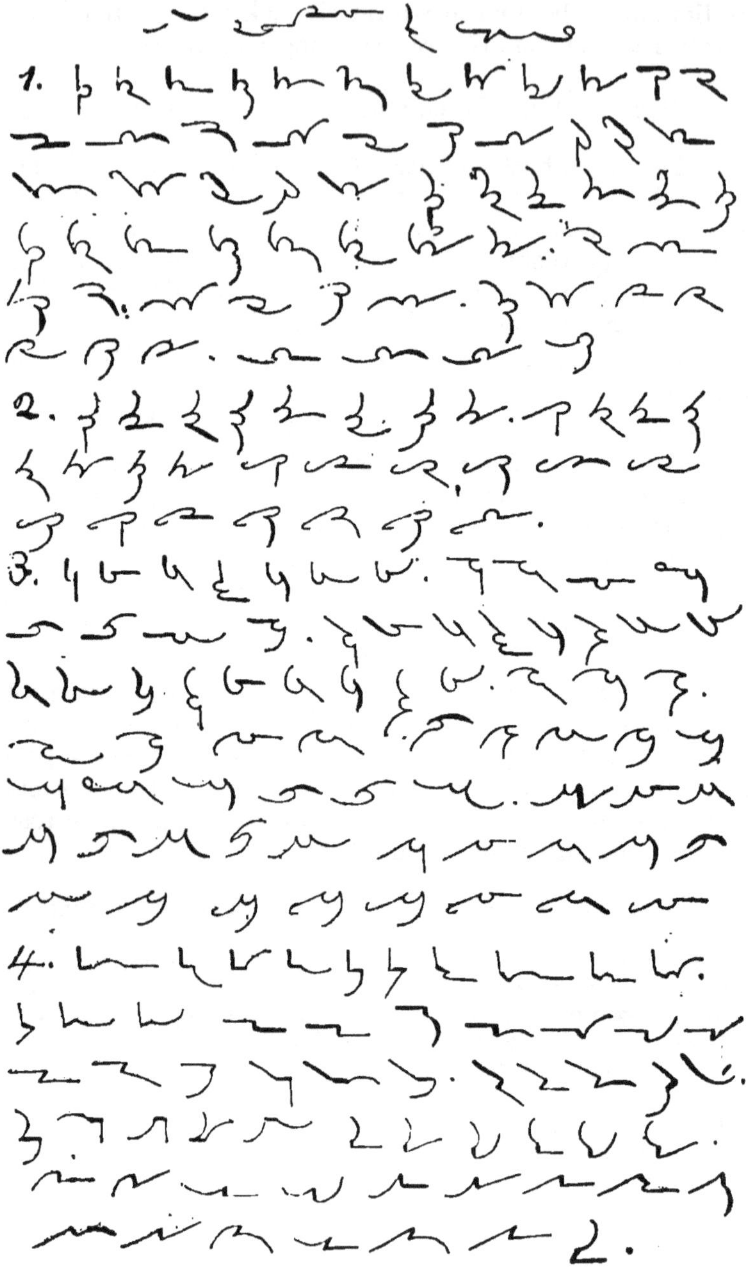
1.
2.
3.
4.

Sec. 9.—Table of Word and Phrase-Signs.

1. Words of one syllable in which the vocal is omitted:

Be been go come can do done to true for form from ever she shall is so us they through thus those am may man many on own or are our we were was you your he her where.

2. Words of one syllable written with vocal signs:

A aye have ah! ye in who all eye high why how out.

3. Words written with contracted vocals:

By boy thy thou my any now new anew few allow.

4. Word-signs variously contracted:

As could should that what had would will which and, etc., head him hath home has does said says some same seen this these then men one once.

5. Derivative word-signs:

Been being upon going doing unto into whose whom also although always having thence thine throughout within without himself yourself herself newness fewness allowance whichever whichsoever whoever whosoever whosesoever whomsoever however howsoever wherever wheresoever whatever whatsoever inform deform reform forming formality informal informality reformatory.

6. Phrase Signs:

I have, I have been, we have been, they have, they have not, they would be, we would have been, we should be, I can, I could, I do, I did, I shall, I am, as well as, as soon as, at last, at once, by chance, do they, to be, to have been, to some, to which, for these, for this, for which, for his, no one, any one, nowhere, anywhere, this is, this was, this will be, in some, in the same, in this, once more, forever, forevermore, forasmuch, forasmuch as, for some, for many, for me, for them, from them, from this time, from such.

First Test Exercise.

1. They came home long ago, not having been absent more than one month. Do they hope to form a company? From whence come those huzzas? They will show them their error. Many a man will eagerly grasp the chance. On no account neglect duty.

"Earth loses thine image forever and aye,
Oh sailor boy, sailor boy, peace to thy soul."

28   A SHORT COURSE

[shorthand content]

IN BUSINESS SHORTHAND 29

[shorthand notation]

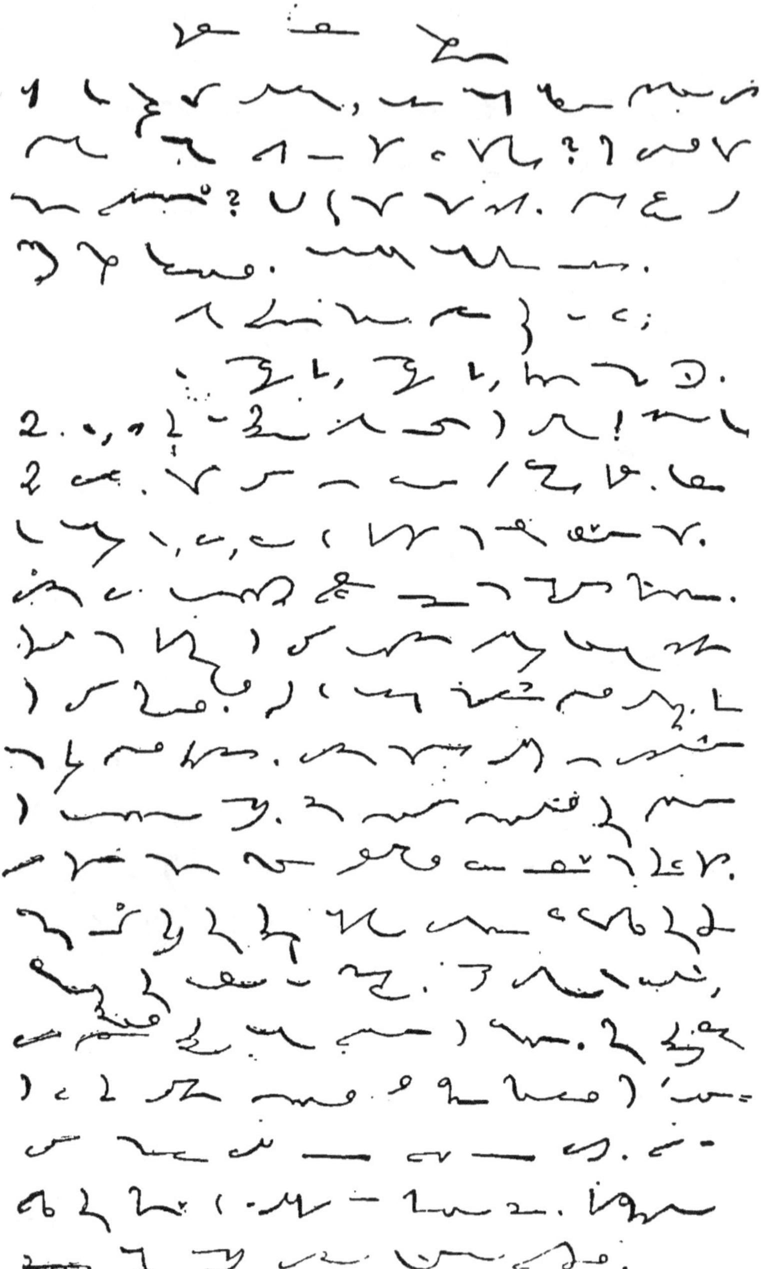

2. Oh! how few and fleeting are the days of youth! how soon they fly away! Come let us anew our journey pursue. They said they neither could, would, nor should perform the task assigned them. With what unseemly haste did the deputy proceed. Follow the perfections of your enemies rather than the errors of your friends. Law should not be the rich man's luxury, but the poor man's remedy. With the many life is one round of unceasing toil. In the solemn silence of the mind are formed those great resolutions which decide the fate of men. Through the dim veil of the visible, and perishing, we get a glimpse of the vast significance of the unseen and eternal. Till we can go alone we must lean on the hand of a guide. From the little stock of a few letters, science has spread branches over all nature. That which you have to do, try to do well. He who hopes for the prize should labor to obtain it. Persevering industry and patient toil win golden harvests.

238 words to be written in 2 minutes and 50 seconds and reduced to 2 minutes and 20 seconds.

Second Test Exercise.

1. We clasify the rocks into stratified and unstratified. He gave express directions and discreet counsels. To him that hath shall be given and he shall have more abundantly, but from him that hath not shall be taken, even that which he seemeth to have. They stroll through the streets and by the side of the stream. They stray on the beach and enjoy the spray of the sea. Spread thy sails, O ship, and speed away. Ascribe majesty to the Most High. Inscribe this maxim on thy heart. A scribe should be a ready writer. We read of those who quenched the violence of fire; out of weakness were made strong; waxed valiant in fight, and turned to flight the armies of the aliens. As soon as they arrive we will inform you of the fact. They have often sought, as we have done, to fathom the depth of this mystery. They ought to have been informed of this measure in time. Wherever we go we see little to exalt, much to depress. No one is so much alone in the world as he who denies God.

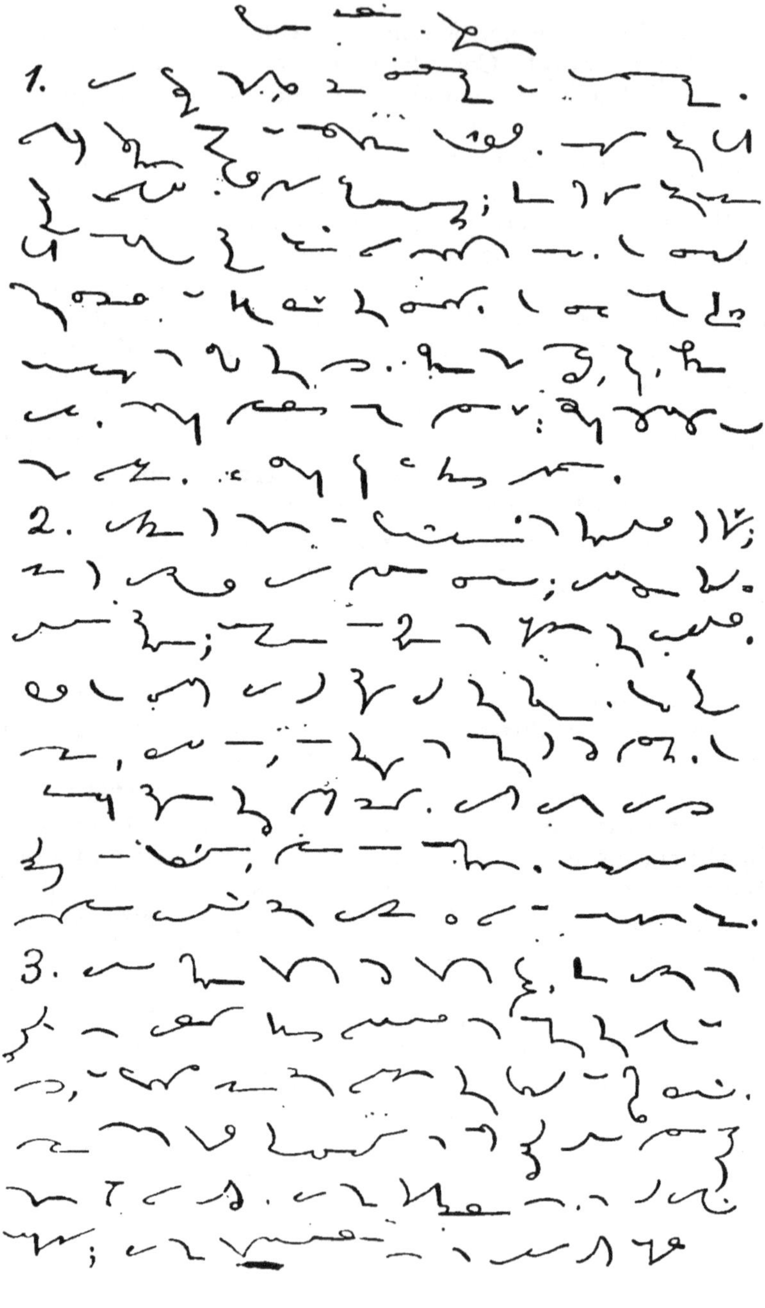

3. When pride cometh, then cometh shame, but with the lowly is wisdom. Beauty haunts the depths of the earth and sea, and gleams out in the hues of the shell and precious stone. Such is the course of nature that whoever lives long must outlive those whom he loves. What thou forbiddest us that will we shun and abhor, what thou commandest us that will we love and pursue.

251 words to be written in 3 minutes and reduced to 2½ minutes.

A student who has a fair command of the simple style should be able to write these test exercises substantially as given on pages 30, 32 and 34, at an average rate of 90 words a minute. The engraved pages may be regarded as a standard of the simple style and the student should be able to write forms at least as briefly as those given. If, however, he has learned other word signs or contractions he need not hesitate to use them. He can safely retain any legitimate form of contraction which he may have previously acquired.

In case he should find his speed grossly deficient or that he is not familiar with the forms of contraction used in the simple style he cannot do better than to take up some elementary work, and perfect himself in that style before proceeding furthe

Third Test Exercise.

1. The Dog in the Manger.

A surly dog had made his way
To a low manger filled with hay;
Here coiled him down, the lazy elf,
And thought of no one but himself.

Hay, corn and fodder neath his paw,
Were not for his rapacious maw.
At last, in came the hungry cow,
Eager to eat the well filled mow.

The barking dog would not give way,—
"Come," quoth the cow, "is this your bay?
You cannot live on cattle's food,
Nor is it for dog's nature good.

"I've wandered long, and now I'm tired;
Nor can I eat till you've retired."—
In vain she begged; the selfish dog
Lay in the manger like a log.

He sought to use the rack in vain,
And took delight in other's pain.—
At last, with well directed horn,
The cow soon tossed him from the corn.

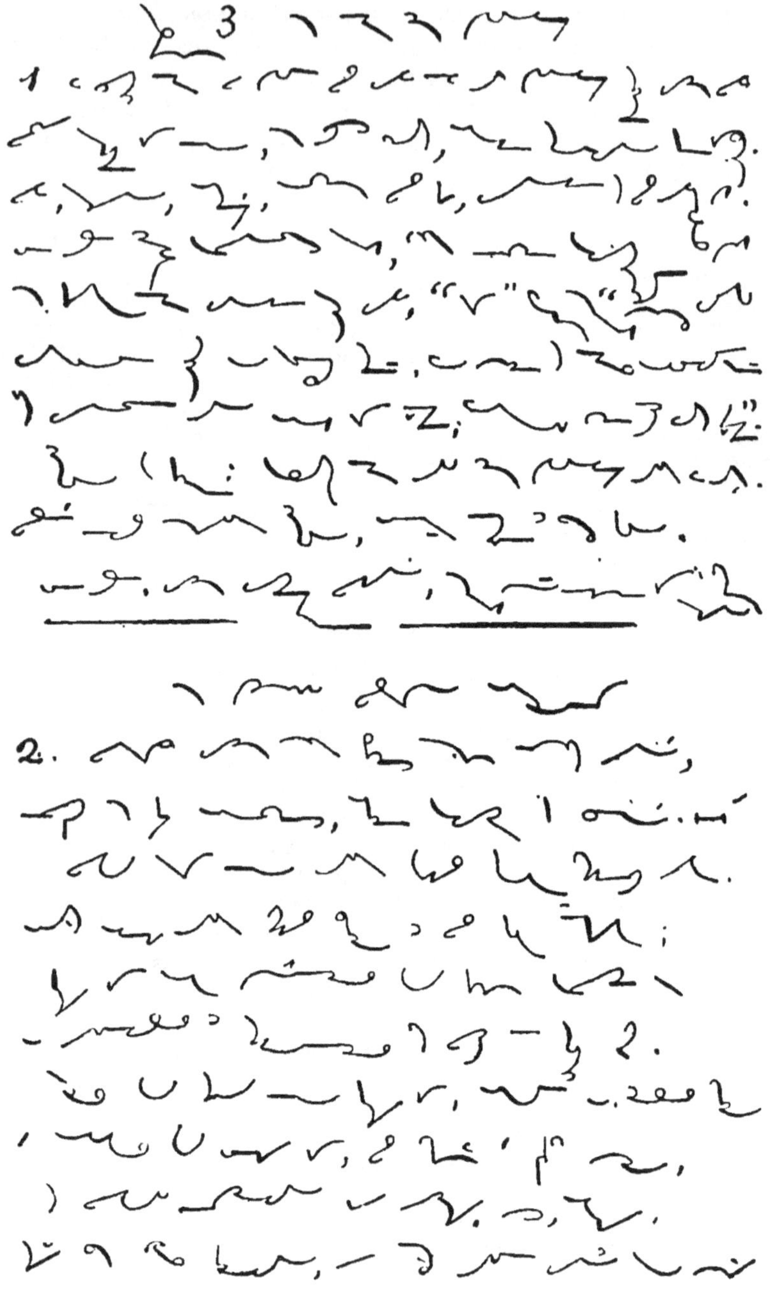

2. THE MESSIAH, HIS COMING AND KINGDOM.

He comes, with succor speedy,
To those who suffer wrong;
To help the poor and needy,
And bid the weak be strong.

He shall come down like showers
Upon the fruitful earth,
And love and joy, like flowers,
Spring in his path to birth;

Before him, on the mountains,
Shall peace, the herald, go,
And righteousness in fountains
From hill to valley flow.

Kings shall fall down before him,
And gold and incense bring;
All nations shall adore him;
His praise all people sing;

For he shall have dominion
O'er river, sea and shore,
Far as the eagle's pinion
Or dove's light wing can soar.

238 words to be written in 2½ minutes and reduced to 2 minutes.

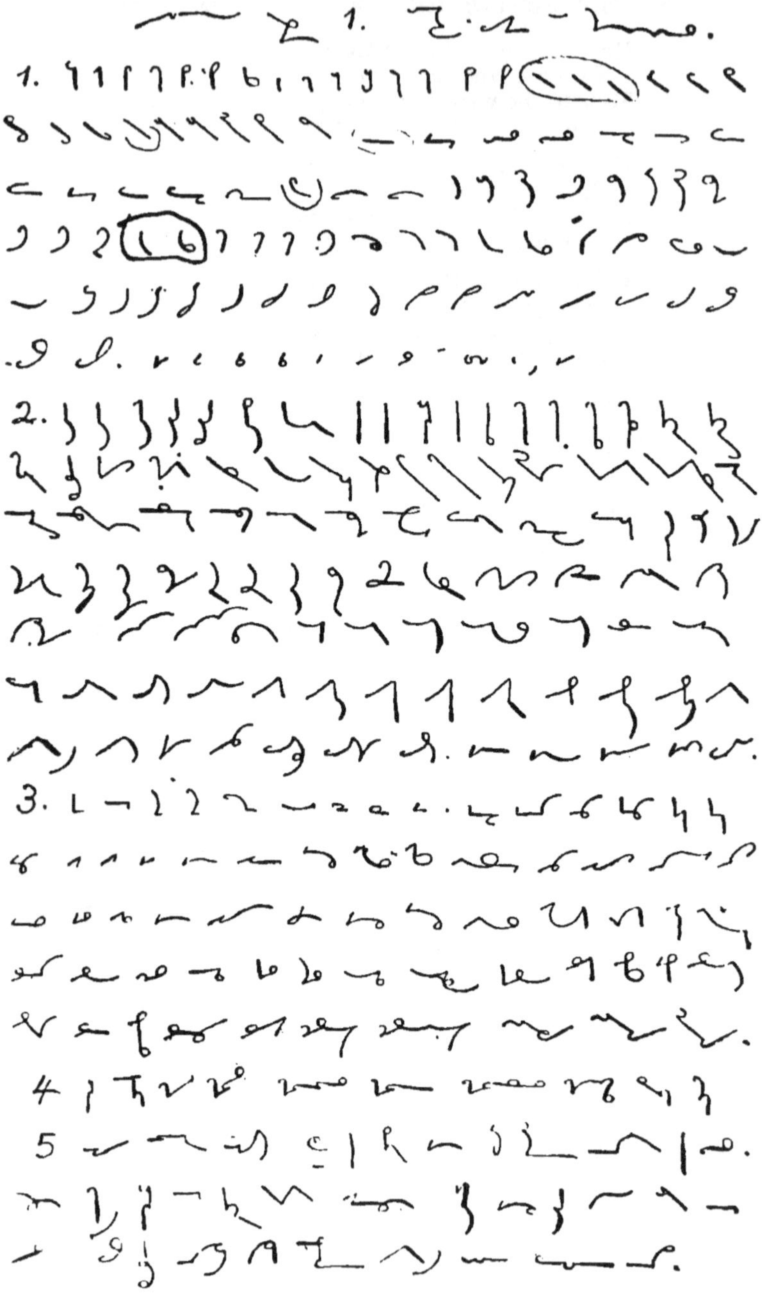

Chapter II.

GENERAL CONTRACTIONS.

Sec. 1. Additional Word Signs.

1. Brief signs are given in the table for the words *the, of, his* and *he,* and ticks for the initial *h* and final *y.*
2. The brief signs for these words are not as available in the Simple Style, because the tick and vocal signs used for *the, he* and *of,* are too fine for that style, and it is desired to distinguish between the *has* and *his.*
3. The tick for *the* should be always joined. It generally ends the phrase, but it may commence it or stand medial. See page 36, Nos. 3 and 4.

(Key to opposite page.)

Writing Excercise 1.

ADDITIONAL WORD AND PHRASE-SIGNS.

1. Above object bill brother subject establish busines but board happy happen opinion principle special stipulate give given together altogether glory signify significance begin began someday account according iniquity school secretary dollar already advertise address take taken tell till almighty general generation each question dwell between very average evening value several half enough satisfy fall full follow advantage advantageous pleasure sure assure official thence think thing thank thanks important importance unless England English alone whole while whilst large least last first most must reply rule with your yours United States, yesterday employ when whence hence he of has the heart.

2. Believe belief objective benevolent benevolence subjective benignant public publish applicable popular purpose probable proper perhaps prospect peculiar pecuniary practice Post Office, perfect prerogative executive begun captain expect collect correct cashier economy character characteristic doctor doctrine descrepancy distinguish displeasure together testify testimony telegraph eternal chapter Vice President, whensoever volume everything overcharge overwhelm Saviour figure forsake favor sufficient falsehood thanksgiving imperfect immediate magazine manufacture manufacturer memoranda memorandum something number neglect never nevertheless November notwithstanding anything honorable like life language represent representative republic republish repugnant respect respective respectively regular regularly reverend remark resemble universaluniform useful employed employing employer employee beyond.

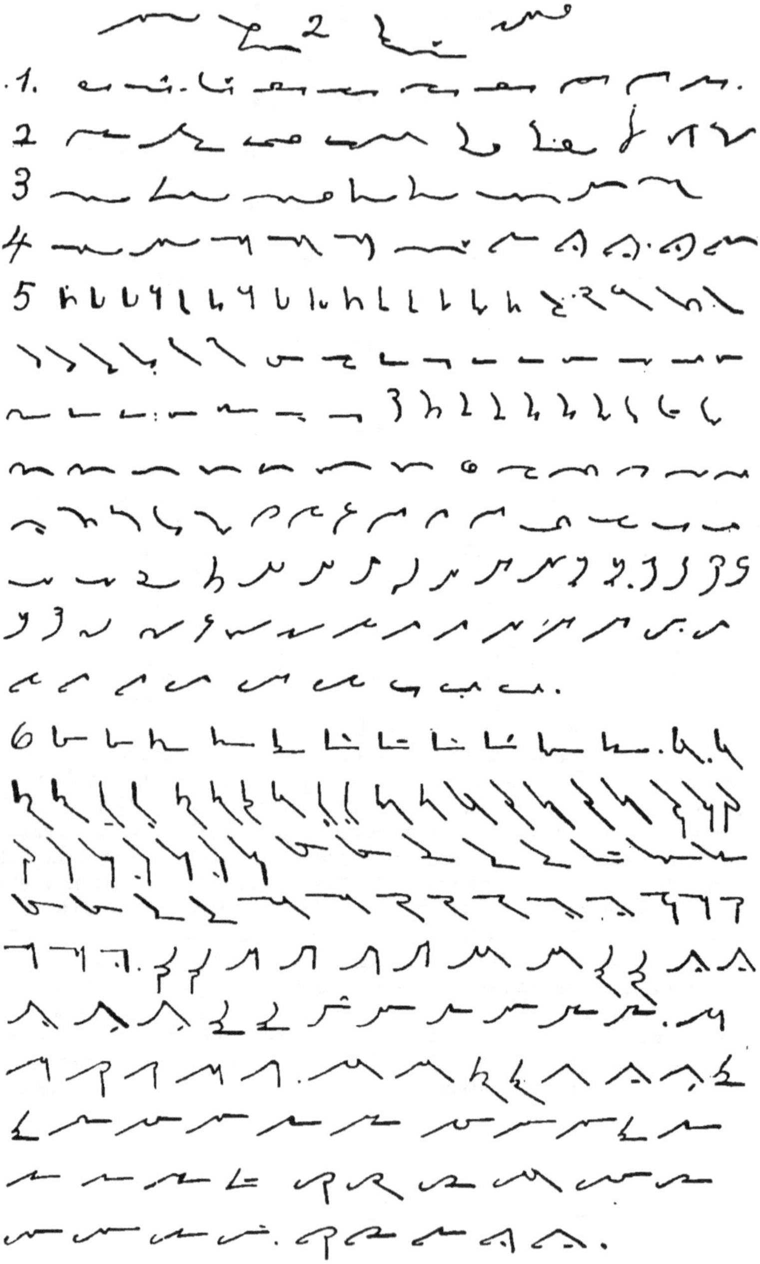
1.
2
3
4
5
6

3. By the, to the, for the, from the, through the, on the, in the, as the, all the, the day, the time, the same, by the same, by and by, by the by, of the same, of the, of all, all of, of us, of which, of this, of these, of business,, of necessity, of some, of one, of many, of me. He does, he has, of his, he is, he was, he says, he sees, he thinks, he knows, he shall be, he may be, he should be, he can be. His time, his own, in his, to his, by his, for his, on his, on his own, by his own, his object, his business, he has been, has never, has come, has done, his purpose, his desire, his error, in his name, in his own name, in accordance with. in account with, in connection with.

4. Board bill, table board, boarder, boarding house, board of directors, board of trade, board of trustees, board of managers, school board, overboard.

5. The way, the truth, and the life. As a popular speaker, he is often invited to make public addresses. This is probably applicable to the peculiar character of the disease, I believe he is a benevolent man. According to the rules of the United States Post Office, the mail must be dispatched regularly, and at stated times.

SEC. 2. A TICK FOR FINAL *y*. INITIAL *h* AND SHORTENED *I*.

A tick slanting backward, as in the word sign *any*, is used for the final *y*, short after the letters *En, Da, Ja, Cha*. Its use on the straight signs is to distinguish the vowel from the en-hook, introduced in a following section.

2. The tick for *h*, contained in the word signs *him, hath*, etc., may be used generally before the letters *De, Ve, Ef, The, Ith, El* and *Em*.

3. The sign for long *I* is shortened by omitting one of the strokes before the letters *En, Es* and *Ze*; as in engraving No. 3.

4. But the alphabetic signs are necessary in many cases for *h* and *i*. See engraving No. 4.

SEC. 3. THE USE OF VOWELS IN WORDS OF ONE SYLLABLE.

1. Words of one consonant stroke not found in the table of Word Signs should be vocalized; though in words like *idea, iota, echo*, etc., all except the first vocal may be omitted. In general the writing of the accented vowel will suffice, as *ba* for *obey, ha* for *aha*.

There are more than a thousand words of one syllable having medial vowels either long or short. For examples see Nos. 5 and 6.

An investigation of the lists given will show that any attempt to write such words with bare skeleton forms is unsatisfactory, for at best the reader will have to guess which one of half a dozen or more words is intended by the outline. These words are treated in this style the same as in the Simple Style; that is, first ·class vowels are joined in the outline, and the dash vowels are also written when long. The vocals generally omitted are the short *u* in *but*, and the *oo* in *book*. For a full treatment of the subject, the student is referred to the Exercise Book, Part 1, and Key, which contain all important words of this class.

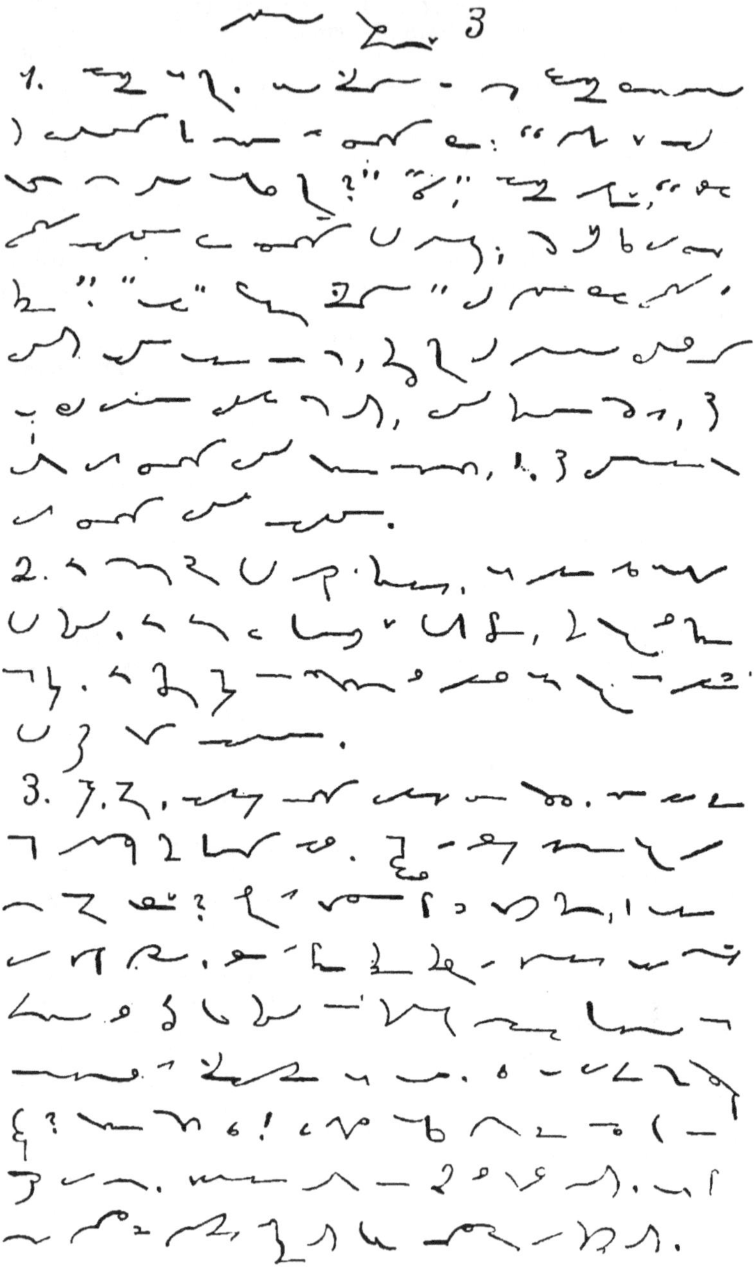

IN BUSINESS SHORTHAND.   41

WRITING EXERCISE 2. VOCALIZED OUTLINES.

1. Sunny downy shiny testy touchy sedgy dusty musty muddy ruddy.
2. Manhood likelihood head-dress hoodwink heaviness half-dozen wholesome humble hither.
3. Sign resign science pine fine nice lies scythe.
4. Dine line type dyke dive size hoed hove hoof hole hoes.
5. Be ba obey abbey bow bough ape pay pa pea poo poe paw pie pew gay eke ache key coo coe caw coy cow oak echo aid day ode dough awed odd add die dew eyed eat oat ought at iota two toe eve fee view few vow avow vie show shoe shy ease easy ooze owes awes eyes ice ace say see saw sigh sue sow thee oath thaw thigh me May aim mow mow mew knee nay gnaw know nigh annoy e'en lea lay la low law lie liew alloy alley oily owl awl eel ale isle ill ell ear air ire our ray row raw rye rue row woo woe hay hoe haw whoa whew whey jaw jew chew.
6. Bate bat beat bet bit boat boot butt bought bite bout bake back beak beck book buck peak peck pick pack poke Puck pike pock. Cake kick keg gig cog cape cap keep kip cope coop cup cob cub cube Kate cat kit coat cot coot kite cute gate gat goat got take tack teak tick talk tuck took tape tap tip top type tub leap lip lap loop lope lop lake lack lick leak leg look luck log lock lead lid led lad load lied lewd loud rape rap reap rip ripe rope rake rack reek rick wreck rook rock read rid red raid ride rode rude rate rat wright writ wrote rot rut route root. Weep weak weed wake weighed wit wide wight wad wood. Heap heed hoed hope hook.

WRITING EXERCISE 3. (See Key.)

1. The Child and the Brook.

An old man who saw a child standing for a long time by the side of a stream, said, "My boy, why do you gaze so long on this brook?" "Sir," the child replied, I stay here to wait till the stream shall run off, then I will pass with dry feet." "Nay," quoth the old man, "you might stay here all your life and yet not do that, for this brook will run on as long as time. And as you wend your way through life, you will find this out. If you go with the stream you will get to the sea, but if you do not go with the stream, you will have to wait."

2. He that soweth iniquity shall reap vanity, and the rod of his anger shall fail. He that hath a bountiful eye shall be blessed, for he giveth his bread to the poor. He that oppresseth the poor to increase his riches, and he that giveth to the rich shall surely come to want. The air, the earth, the water, teem with joy at existence. The idea of what ought to be rises up from the bosom of what is. The pages of history! how is it that they are so dark and sad? He spoke of the homestead bill in homely phrase, but not with humble mien. He said he plead for it for the sake of humanity and would sooner resign his office than fail to furnish such a benison to the denizens of the old world and the new. Whence, and what art thou

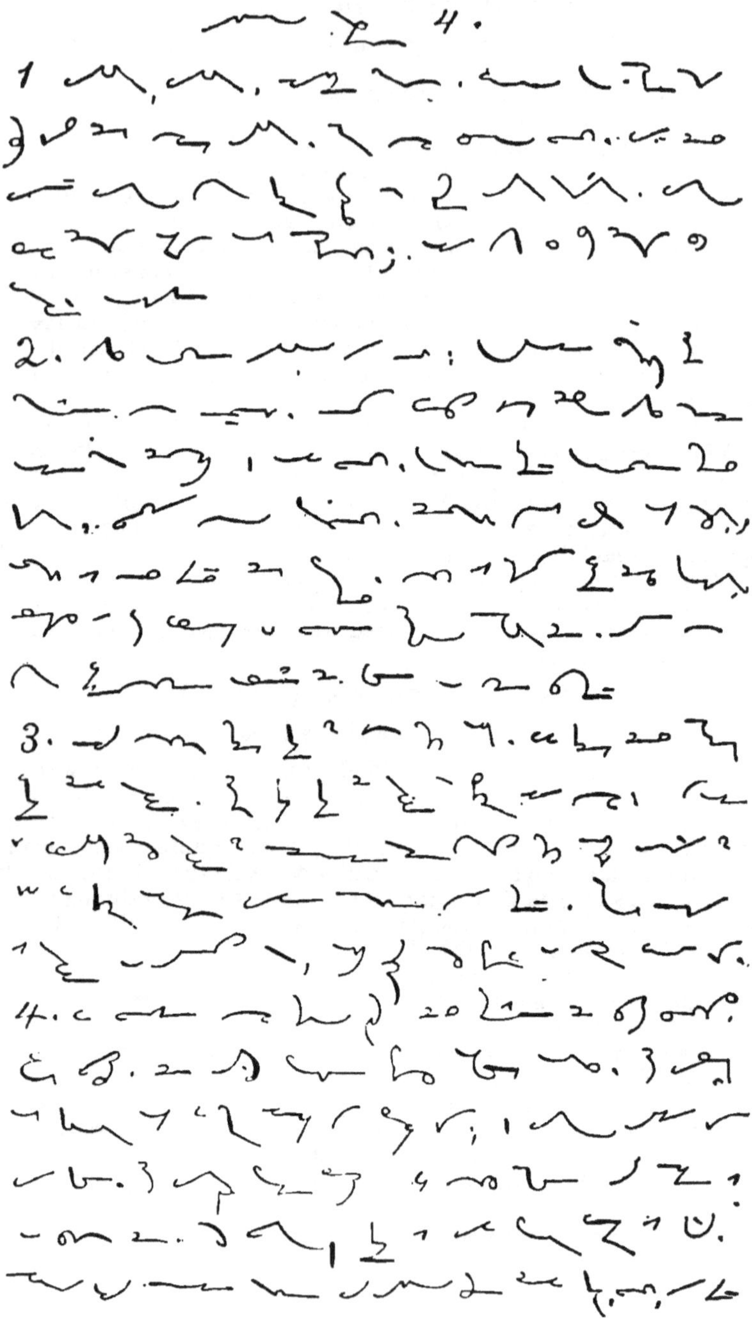

execrable shape? Get thee hence! When he comes on business, make it to his advantage to deal with us. I would not like to follow his course of life. No subject is of more importance in the morality of private life than that of domestic or family life.

323 words to be written in 3½ minutes and reduced to 2½ minutes.

WRITING EXERCISE 4.

1. Wake, wake, the wild echoes! Anon they dip their facile oars into the sedgy lake. The oak is a strong tree; with its wood we can make big ships that float like cork. We can stay in them and roam on the deep sea; and we may be as safe in them as in a coach on the road.

2. Herbs need rain or dew; they will not thrive if the ground is too dry. Tom tells me he saw, in the south, herbs that did not grow in the soil, but on a tree. They get the food they need from its bark. Here is an oak tree, it grew many years ago near this rock and threw out its roots into the clefts. See how firm a hold it has upon the rock. The storms of half a century have tried in vain to shake it. Let us make a rude seat, and sit in the shade, and eat some food.

3. Do you see that pretty bird, he is free and happy. What a pity it is to shut up a bird in a cage. If that poor bird in the cage could speak, he would say: "Am not I a slave in this cage? Did not God make me free to fly and soar? I have a beak and claws with which to get my food. Open the door of the cage, and let me go, and I will leave this place and seek a new home.".

4. A trout is a fine fish. It is found in the small streams among the hills. It loves quiet places and shady nooks. If we step on the bank near a brook the jar may scare him, but we can lure him with bait if we keep quite still. When he sees the bait, he will dart out and seize it, then he can be pulled out with a quick jerk of the pole. Take care that you do not get your line fast in a bush, tree or root.

344 words to be written in 3½ minutes and reduced to 2¾ minutes.

WRITING EXERCISE 5.

(See engraving.)

1. Allow me to ask you to copy this paper, copy it first in Takigrafy. See that you do it correctly. Did you say you would do so? Oh, yes, I hear you now; thank you. Let thy yea be yea, and thy nay, nay. As we sow, so shall we reap. Do you know of any man who has no foe? Put that load of hay upon the mow, now go and hoe the peas. Why do you do so? How could they think of such a thing? I will show you how to do the work. Do you get the idea? This will aid you to add to your store of knowledge. They should pay a fee for such service.

2. If they annoy you they may go away. The way of a man is right in his own eyes. We, you, he, and they were there. Each of

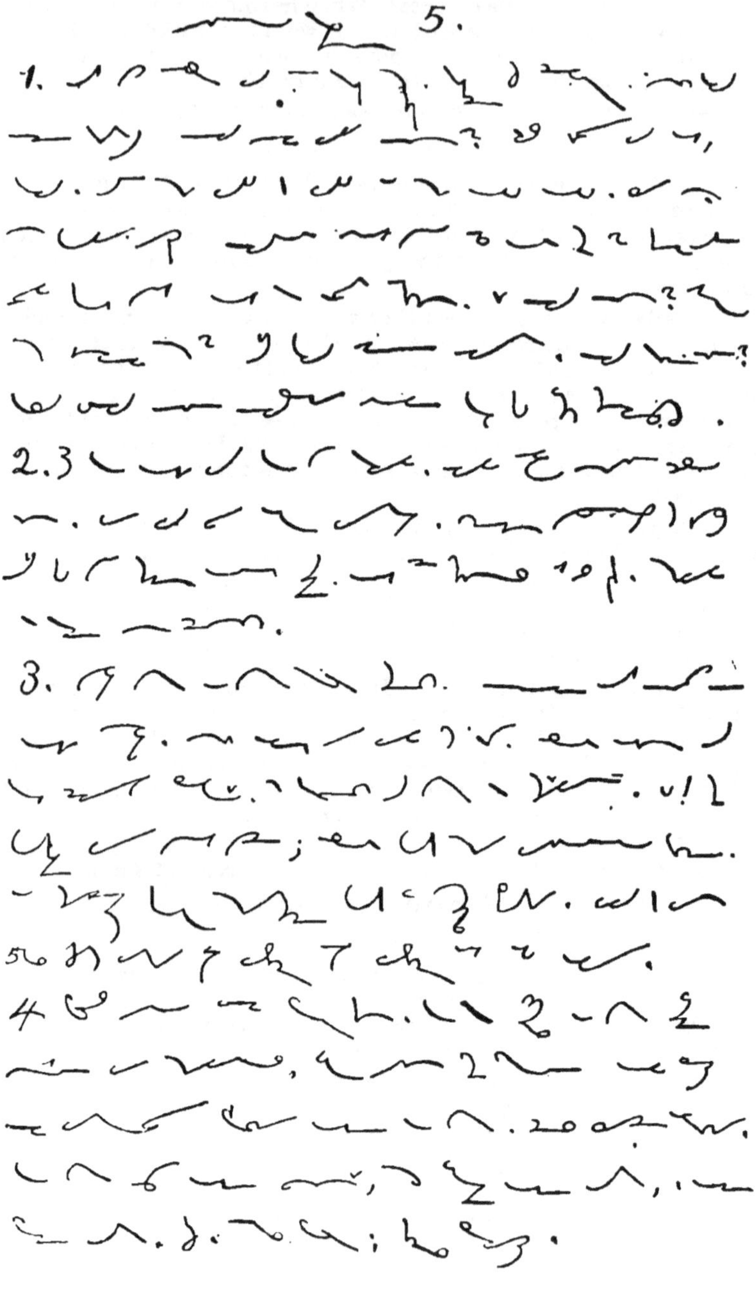

us must answer for himself. I will pay my vows unto the Lord now in the presence of all His people. Thy way, O God, is in the sea.
3. Mary may go and make cake for tea. Do not allow Tommy to annoy Sarah. Sue and Joe are away from home. The snow and ice will thaw in the warm sunshine. That oak tree will make good fire wood.

Ah! few shall part where many meet,
The snow shall be their winding sheet,
And every turf beneath their feet
Shall be a soldier's sepulcher.

Would you be wise, five things observe with care; of whom you speak, to whom you speak, and how, and when, and where.
4. Quails run at a quick pace. They go in flocks, and make a loud sound with their wings. When they rise from the ground on a still day we can hear the queer note they make. It is sweet and clear. They make the same note twice, then a third note like, but not quite like the first. Ducks quack, pigs squeal.

334 words to be written in 3¼ minutes and reduced to 2¼.

SEC. 4. WORDS OF A SINGLE STEM CONTAINING SIGNS OF THE L, R, QUA, AND CIRCLE SERIES.

Words of a single stem containing signs of the L. R, Qua, and circle series are also vocalized, unless especially excepted. So also words having an initial vowel. See page 46, Nos. 1 and 2.

SEC. 5. EXTENDED USE OF THE COMPOUNDS OF THE L AND R SERIES.

The rule directing that compounds of the L and R series should always exclude the vowel must be carefully observed; but some exceptions are allowed for convenience sake in which the vowel is included, The most useful words in this class are given in No. 3.

REM. The cases in which the compound sign may include the vocal need not be rigidly limited to the above list. But the student should be extremely cautious how he adds to it, and not fall into the slovenly habits of the Phonographic writers, who, in their use of these compounds, know no method and no law, and reap as a result a system of outlines extremely illegible and confusing.

SEC. 6. THE USE OF ZHE FOR JA AND NJ.

Zhe may be written for *Ja* or *nj*, as in the words given in No. 4.
The signs for *Zhl Shl* and *Zhr Shr* are also used in a few instances for *jl chl* and *jr chr* as given in No. 5. The full form is sometimes prefered. In some cases the contracted form might be misread, as, pusher for pitcher; washer for watcher. If this form of contraction is used in *soldier*, *verdure*, *etc.*, it should be noted that these outlines do not convey the exact pronunciation, which is *sold-yer*, *verd-yer*.

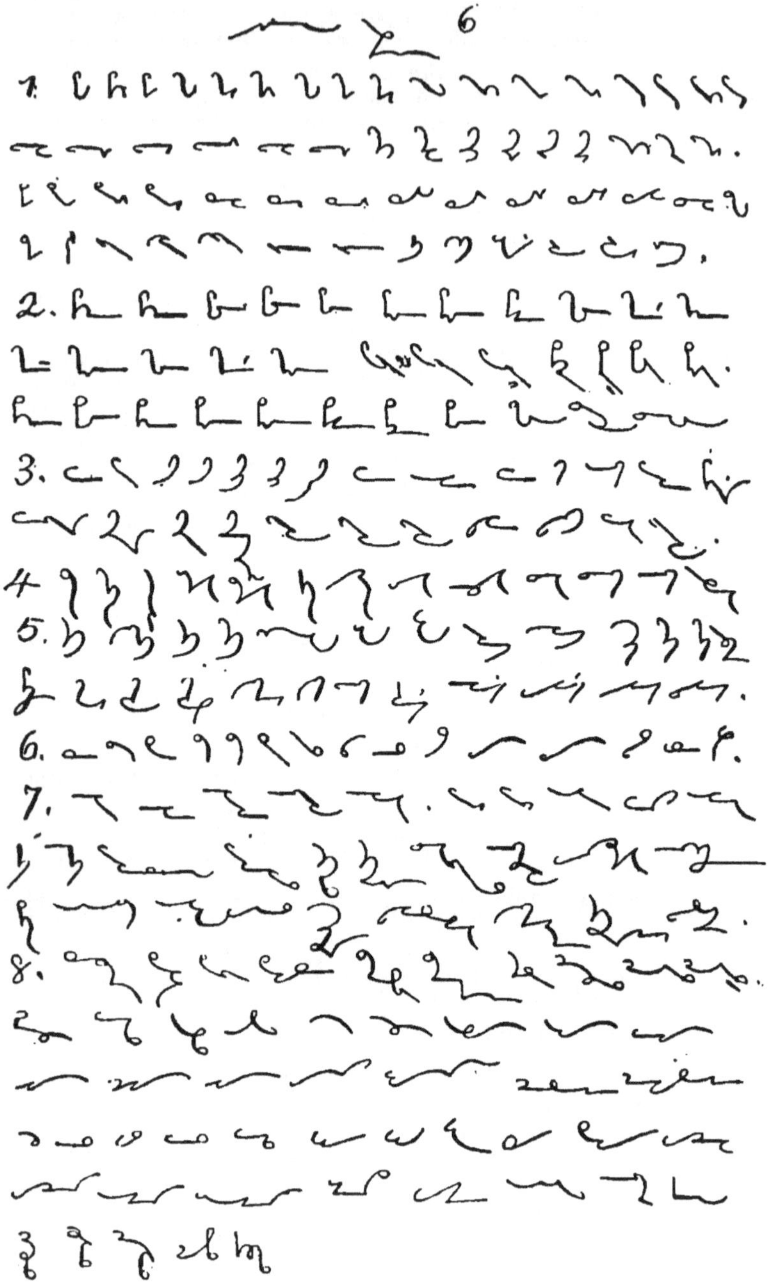

IN BUSINESS SHORTHAND. 47

SEC. 7. THE USE OF THE CIRCLE WHERE THE VOCAL IS INCLUDED.

The circle in its first and proper use is designed to indicate the exclusion of the vocal; so its use in such words as *this* and *these*, given in the table of word-signs, and *set, saith, south, save*, etc., given in No. 6, p. 46 are exceptional. Such exceptions should be limited to the examples given, or to other words of frequent occurence carefully selected, and the general rule should be observed in all other cases.

WRITING EXERCISE 6.

1. Play plea ply bray brow brew pray pry prow gray agree cry crew grow glow glee claw dray dry draw drew tray try free fray flee fly flow flew three throw threw spy sky skew scow stay stow stew slay slow sly slew sway stray spray spry. Opal ochre eagle eager odor utter awful evil azure owner only idle.

2. Pleat plead plate played plaid plight plied plowed. Braid broad bread brood bride brad brought bright. Quake quack quick. Speak spoke spake spike speed spade sped spied spite spout spit spat sprain screen strain.

3. Dull call full fill fulfil folly fully till until tell. Sure ensure college pilgrim telegram fulcrum vulgar Philadelphia garner corner colonel mortal martial nourish kernel.

4. Savage privilege vegetable average suffrage beverage revenge arrange disarrange strange stranger danger exchange.

5. Official ambrosial vigil fragile essential agile angel cudgel satchel soldier verdure perjure exaggerate plagarism journey journal journalism majority measure treasure pitcher ditcher watcher archer searcher.

6. Set saith south save safe sake case some days less ways wise house aside assume.

ADDITIONAL PHRASE SIGNS.

7. To call, to tell, to college, to garner, to nourish, call out, call in, on call, tell me, until they, be sure, to be sure, college student, college class, official business, official notice, strange occurence, danger signal, woman suffrage, Teacher's Institute, as a beverage, on an average, on angel wings, Soldier's Home, Merchant's Exchange, majority vote, Vigilance Committee, house and lot.

8. Sets forth, South America, South Carolina, South-west, Saving's Bank, Safe Deposit, for the sake of, in this case, in any case, in no case, in all cases, which shows, this shows, less than, more than, this is, this was, that was, which was, all ways, in all ways, he was, wise man. a wise man, it is not, it was not, that is, it is, what is, which is, which has, when we, when you, when they, as we, as they were, one day, one time, any time, at any time, at all times, one or two, now and then, to and fro, up and down, in the first place, in the second place, in the third place, in the last place, peace principles.

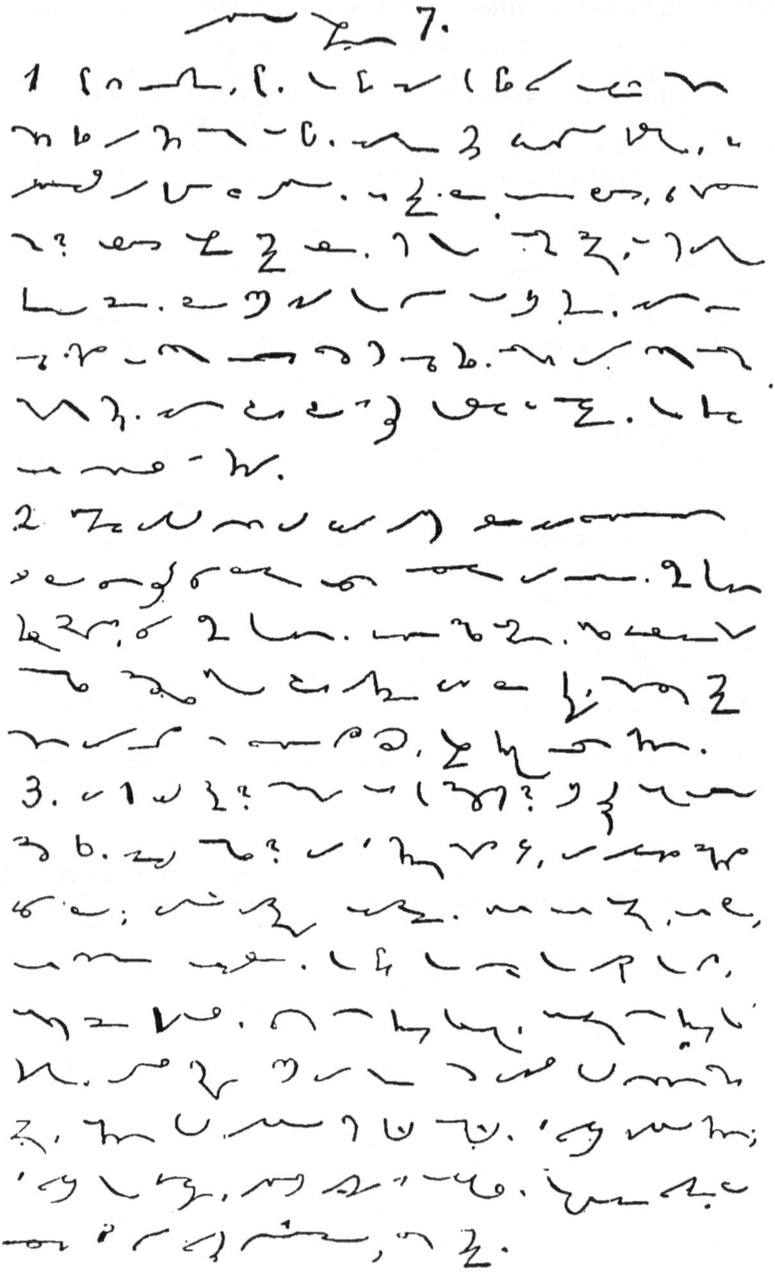

Writing Exercise 7.

1. Blow ye the trumpet, blow! They ply the oar. She plies her needle. Those three boys are free to go and play. The wicked flee when no man pursueth, but the righteous are bold as a lion. And the Lord said unto Satan: whence comest thou? And Satan answered the Lord and said: From going to and fro in the earth, and from walking up and down in it. In an evil hour they met an awful fate. He was true to his promise and eager to draw others over to his views. The crew were eager to throw the cargo overboard. He was the only owner of the vessel. They will stay a day or two. They betray no signs of fear.

2. I dare say we shall see you when we arrive. He said he would try to do so. His son says he will sell some stock and cease to struggle with debt. Save the pennies, for the sake of economy, sir, save the pennies. The tide ebbs and flows. I guess he does not care to do this. In this case I can only repeat what I said before. Thus saith the Lord. Those were times that tried men's souls. These are the piping days of peace.

3. What object have you in view? Is there any advantage in this measure? I will leave nothing undone in this business. How do you do this? We all breath the common air, we rejoice in the beams of the same sun, we own one father and one God. I know no North, no South, no East, no West. They plow, they sow, they reap, they mow and gather into barns. Something is better than nothing, and anything is better than everything. Let us overcome evil with good, then wars shall cease throughout the earth and peace shall reign from pole to pole. All hail the reign of peace. All hail King of Salem, rightful ruler of all nations. They shall not hurt nor destroy in all my holy mountain, saith the Lord.

312 words to be written in 3½ minutes and reduced to 2¼ minutes.

Writing Exercise 8.

1. Speak the piece I pray thee as I pronounce it to thee. No man can make a good plea for a dram. We have green peas on a plate in the month of July. Sheep bleat when they wish to call their lambs. The azure vault of heaven, which we call the sky, is blue. Call a spade a spade. Do your duty; fulfill your mission; be a man among men. The duck said quack, quack, quack; the Duke said quick, quick, quick. They quake with fear. What he thought an opal, was found to be a piece of yellow ochre.

2. Eternal vigilence is the price of liberty. This, as an initial measure, is essentially necessary to our design. He gave official notice of his desire to visit us. As both teacher and preacher, he deserves special mention. The soldiers are glad to escape the dangers of battle, and return to the peaceful walks of life. Be sure you're right, then go ahead. Bunyan wrote the Pilgrim's Progress and the Holy War.

8.

1.

2.

3.

4.

IN BUSINESS SHORTHAND. 51

3. The college boy sends a telegram to his father in Philadelphia. This will be very likely to fill our reasonable demands. That savage attack was in revenge for what he thought a personal injury. Truth is stranger than fiction. The vulgar crowd delight in martial music. No man is always wise.

4. This is no strange occurrence. We met him at the teacher's institute where he spoke for woman-suffrage. He said he never took alcoholic liquors as a beverage. He will travel through the South-west, and go to Mexico and South America for the sake of increasing his knowledge of botany. This shows that he is a lover of science. Having bought a house and lot, he was chosen cashier of the Saving's Bank, and an officer in the Vigilance Committee. He said they would make rum an outlaw by a majority vote on the next election day.

320 words to be written in 3½ minutes and reduced to 2½ minutes.

SEC. 8. SHORTENED LETTERS.

1. The letters *d* and *t* unite without a vowel with all consonant sounds except themselves, as in the words *that, apt, east, eased, ant, and, art, hard, etc.* It will be observed that the light letter unites only with *t*, and the heavy letter with *d*. So we have this rule: A light letter may be written half length to imply a *t*, and a heavy letter to imply a *d*. The liquids, *el, em, en* and *ar*, form an exception to this rule, since they unite with both *t* and *d*; as in the examples above, and when shortened to imply *d*, the shortened letter is shaded.

2. A half-length letter cannot be joined to a full length letter unless it makes with it, or with a proper vocal, a definite angle. Where no angle can be formed, both letters must be written in full.

3. There are some exceptions to the rule requiring that the light letters indicate only *t*, and heavy letters only *d*, in such word signs as *but, great, that, could, should, etc.*, and in some longer words, but the rule should be insisted on.

4. The half-length principle applies also to the final compounds of the *l* and *r* series.

REM. For further instruction in the use of the half-length signs, see Chapter III.

WRITING EXERCISE 9. SHORTENED LETTERS.

Use half length signs in:

1. Blabbed grabbed stabbed apt tapped capped wrapped lapped act tacked backed packed lacked dipped tipped sipped tripped bagged dragged gagged wagged dogged ticked tricked strict talked balked aft draft graft craft shaft laughed raft drift gift sift lift loft soft left bereft lived loved saved raved abashed dashed cashed lashed brushed blushed crushed rushed washed wreathed breathed

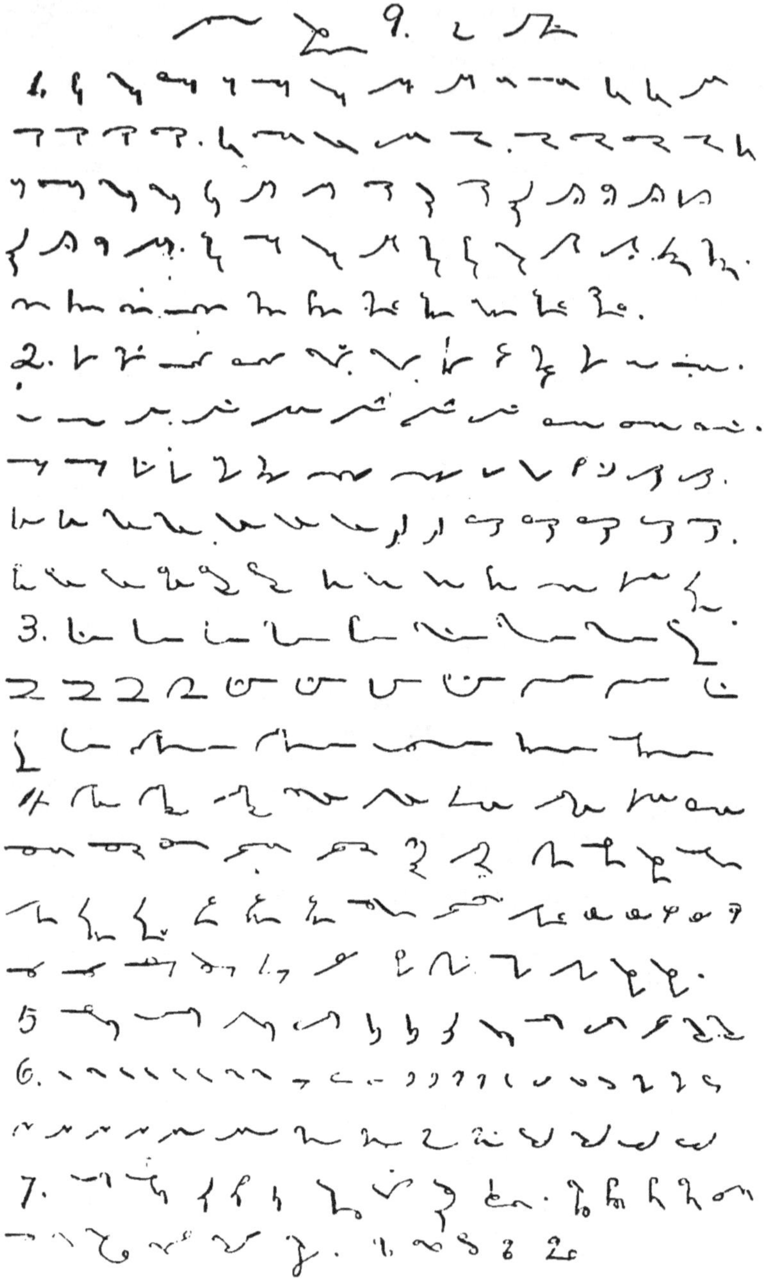

IN BUSINESS SHORTHAND.

east beast eased teased priest pleased praised abused accused abased effaced.

2. Pumped prompt tempt stemmed cramped crammed hemmed aimed framed formed aunt daunt end tend lend loaned rained round hound wound stand strand stoned tart tarred port poured afford feared seared soured oared gored soared old willed wilt paint pained grant grand gained caned canned build built stilt stilled steeled chilled drilled spanned scanned scant sprained screened skinned. Bind (bond) kind (conned) grind blind (blonde) signed remind refined.

Full length letters are used in:

3. Boned bound pound brunt blunt groaned crowned ground gloved dealt dulled sold mould shield shelled belt quelled mound mount showed shoved shunned emblazoned imprisoned unseasoned peasant unpleasant.

Additional shortened forms:

4. Implant imprint reprint ingrained regained retained refrained remained sustained distract district instruct retract restrict inflict reflect imposed disposed exposed enclosed reposed refused revised amazed amused aroused disgraced retraced replaced ascend assent assort assert insert desert desired distort extort retort resort support import deport report export expert.

5. Discovered endeavored recovered wavered beveled baffled leveled gathered tethered weathered rumored garnered cornered.

6. Good great glad gold called cold card court doubt told toward fort felt short assured shut yet cannot, could not, bright fright quite might light right write writing lighten brighten frighten shorten shorthand culture courtier nature nurture.

7. On board, on ship board, larboard, star-board, bed and board, gold basis, gold mine, gold and silver, postal card, court of common pleas, police court, superior court, supreme court, circuit court, district court, court of quarter sessions, court house, court yard, court plaster, as broad as, as great as, as good as, as short as, as shrewd as.

WRITING EXERCISE 10.

1. He assumed an air of great superiority. They affect to despise small things. Reflect on your ways and reject all doubtful schemes. Respect and love your parents and friends. Act well thy part there all the glory lies. If we would not like to be frightened or deceived ourselves, it cannot be right to frighten or deceive others. Aright, aloft, above, below, he whirled the rapid sword. Measure your life by acts of goodness not by years. It is the duty of a child not to direct but to obey his parents. The region beyond the grave is not a solitary land. Sincere respect for the men of early

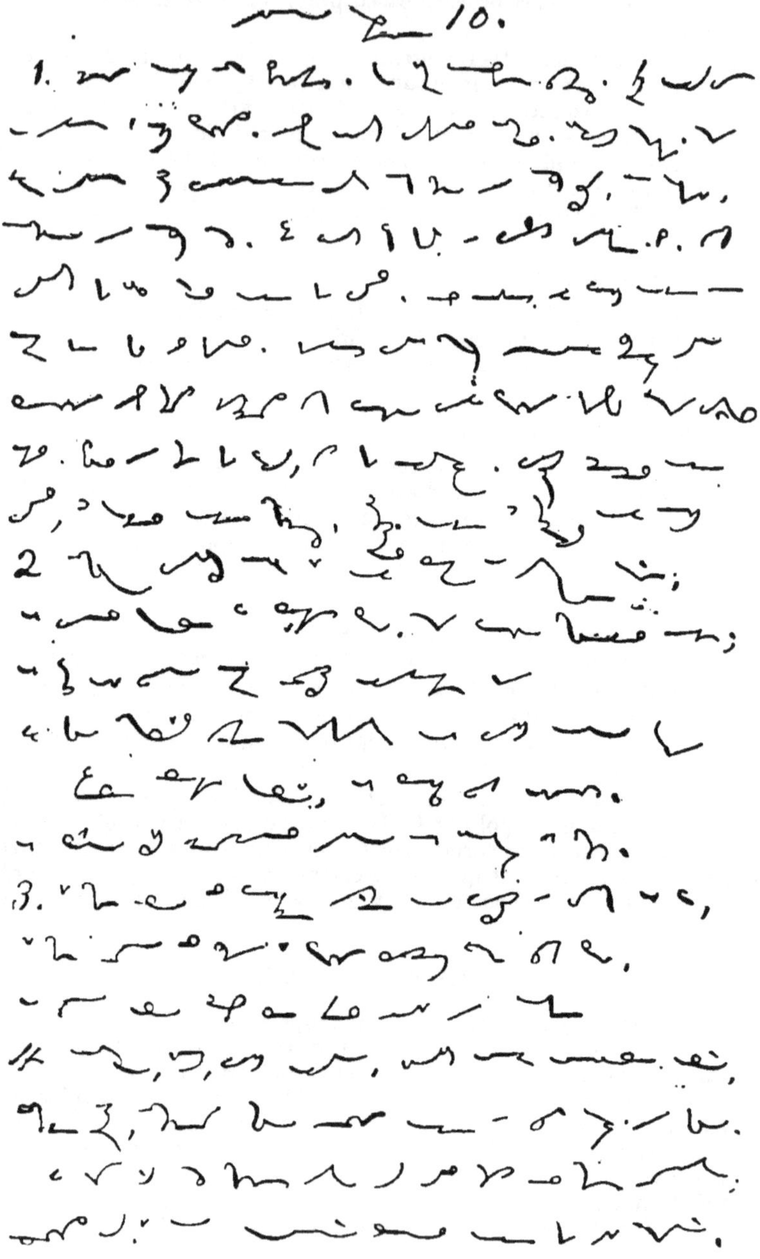

times may be joined with a clear perception of their weaknesses and errors. Plants are formed by culture, men by education. We live in deeds not years, in thoughts not breaths, in feelings not in figures on a dial.

2. The breaking waves dashed high on a stern and rock bound coast,
And the woods 'gainst a stormy sky their giant branches tossed,
And the heavy night hung dark, the hills and waters o'er;
When a band of exiles moored their bark, on the wild New England shore.
Amid'st the storm they sang, and the stars heard, and the sea,
And the sounding isles of the dim woods rang to the anthem of the free.

3. I praised the sun whose chariot rolled on wheels of amber and of gold,
I praised the moon whose softer eye gleams sweetly through the summer sky,
And moon and sun in answer said our days of light are numbered.

4. Unthinking, idle, wild, and young, I laughed, and talked, and danced, and sung,
And proud of health, of freedom vain, dreamed not of sorrow, care or pain.
When I am old, this breezy earth will lose for me its voice of mirth;
The streams will have an undertone of sadness, not by right their own.

318 words to be written in 3¼ minutes, and reduced to 2½ minutes

Sec. 9. Lengthened Curves.

1. The letters *Ef, Ve, Ish, Ev, Ze, Em, En* and *El* are made twice their usual length to imply an additional *tr*, as in the words *after enter*, and the lengthened *En* and *El* are shaded to imply *dr*, as in *under, elder*.

Notice that this form of contraction is used where no vowel occurs between the three letters indicated by the lengthened stem, though a vowel may follow the first letter as in the words *matter, lighter*.

This contraction does not apply when a vowel follows the *r*. The lengthened curve can be used in *literal*, but not in *lottery*. See examples of the use of the lengthened curves in exercise 11, Nos. 1 and 3, and examples in No. 2 where other forms of contraction are preferred.

2. The letters *Qua* and *Twa* are lengthened to imply *tr*, as in *equator, twitter*, and the lengthened *qua* may be shaded to imply *dr*, as in *quadruped, quater* may be written for *quarter*. See No. 5.

11.

IN BUSINESS SHORTHAND. 57

The letter *Em* is lengthened to imply *tr* when light, but the lengthened *Em* when shaded implies *br* and *pr*, as in *ember, tamper*. See No. 6.

The letters *The* and *Ith* are lengthened to imply *r*,* the lenghened *Ith* indicating *there* (expletive) and the lengthened *Ath there* (adverb) and *their;* though in phrases, these signs are, for convenience, interchanged. The *The* is lengthened to express the word *other*, with an initial *E* the word *either*, and with a preceding tick the word *whether*.

Notice that the words *there* (expletive), *there* (adverb), and *their*, are written with light signs through the "th" is really semi-vocal.

The letter *En* is made treble length to imply "thr" in the words *neither, another*. This sign may be used also in such words as *misanthropy, anthropology*. The *Ing* is also trebled in the words *stronger, longer, younger*.

KEY TO WRITING EXERCISE 11.
(Use the lengthened curves.)

1. Fetter fitter fighter after laughter rafter lifter sifter softer refitter fritter fretter flutter flatter voter provider invader divider shutter shatter Easter oyster boaster poster blister bluster piaster plaster Gloucester cloister duster toaster jester fester fluster shyster moister roster foster disaster sister suiter seeder seceder cider hard cider soft-sodder cider-mill minister.

2. Setter sadder Chester Colchester Dorchester Manchester pester chorister barrister forester songster luster lustrous illustrious industrious distress sinister monster.

3. Matter mutter smatter smiter diameter hexameter letter litter loiter lighter slaughter insulter defaulter filter elder older milder moulder wilder wilderness bewilder balder builder smolder shelter shoulder.

4. Under sunder enter center ponder banter canter winter hinder tender pretender defender sender thunder binder Alexander render wonder yonder slendor collender provender lavender inventor.

5. Equator twitter quarter quarter-section Quarter-master quadruped quadrumane quadruple.

6. Member ember remember timber temper distemper bumper scamper pamper clamber cumber encumber lumber September December temperance, temperance society, temperance principles, intemperance.

7. There there their either other otherwise wether whether whither rather author therefore thereof therein thereon their own, by their, with their, on their, the other day, the other way, in there, if there s, if it is, if it was.

*The use of the lengthened *The, Ith, Thu, Ath,* to add *r* instead of *tr* is here introduced into Takigrafy for the first time. It has, however, received a measure of consideration on the part of the author for the past two or three years, and is believed to provide improved signs for the words affected by it.

12.

8. Another neither misanthropy anthopology, in no other way, in another way, in neither way, in some other way, at other times, at another time, at no other time, at some other time.

9. Longer younger stronger, longer time, longer than, younger years, years old, years of age, so soon, so easy, so many, so far as, so much as, as much as, for as much as, as far as, as fast as, as large as, as long as, as little as, as soon as, as safe as, as strong as, as straight as, as low as, as high as, as slow as.

WRITING EXERCISE 12.

1. They flatter the foreign invader. He is a good provider. After a long fit of laughter they proceed to consult the meter. The forester says the weather is milder in the wilderness than in the open field. The officer caught the prize-fighter and put him in fetters. He said in his letter that he was a voter, and did not care to fritter away his influence. The railroad disaster was the cause of great slaughter. He is not only a defaulter, but an insulter of the majesty of the law, and hopes to be an eluder of its penalties. The older of the two is an elder in the church, a builder by trade.

2. In entering upon the winter, the couple determined, with silly banter, to part asunder for a season, but Alexander was more tender, and said he would not be a pretender, but would be her defender. He had been led to ponder upon how he could render more assistance from his slender income.

3. We often have thunder in the month of November, very seldom in December. The member said he could not remember anything about the collender. They do not dare to tamper with the timber. The doctors say they can arrest the distemper, but prescribe strict temperance; we must be temperate in eating, temperate in drinking, temperate in working, and avoid all intemperate action.

4. There, there, are the friends of other days! The author said he would go whether the weather was good or otherwise. Having read therein and thought thereon, I know whereof I speak, therefore can speak thereof with assurance. There is a God: the herbs of the valley, the cedars of the mountains bless him; insects sport in his beams, the elephant salutes him with the rising orb of day, the bird sings him in the foliage, the thunders proclaim him in the Heavens, the ocean declares his immensity; man alone has said, "There is no God." The heavens and earth, O Lord, proclaim thy boundless power. The soul of man is larger than the sky, deeper than the ocean, or the abyssmal dark of the the unfathomed center.

354 words to be written in 4 and reduced to 2¾ minutes.

SEC. 10. MISCELLANEOUS CONTRACTIONS.

All modes of contraction in Takigrafy are designed to indicate the exclusion of the vowel from the portion of the word so contracted. Fully written alphabetic forms in general indicate the presence of the vowel. Where two or more sounds unite without a vowel, their union is generaly indicated by some modification of one of the letters.

13

(shorthand exercises)

IN BUSINESS SHORTHAND.

This is done in the use of both the initial and final circle, and in compounds having initial hooks, as well as in the shortened and lengthened forms given in the preceeding lessons. There are a few other modes of contraction expressing the exclusion of a vowel between the consonants, which are applicable, however, to only a few letters. Those given in this lesson are: 1, the n-hook; 2, the v-hook; 3, the shaded Em implying p: 4, the shaded Ar implying j and cha; 5, the shaded El implying r, and 6 the shaded Ra implying l; all of which are illustrated on page 60.

Notice that the n-hook is on the left and under side of the straight stems, and is enlarged to form the v-hook. The right hand small hook expresses an, and enlarged ain. Notice further that the use of the Emp, Arch, Arj, Ler and Rel are limited to words in which the implied letters are in the same syllable with the shaded stroke, and that the full forms are always allowable, and often preferred. In general, the student will do well to use these contractions only in the words given in the exercises.

SEC. 11. THE STE AND EST LOOPS.

A small loop is used both initially and finally for *st*; the initial loop is named Ste, the final Est. They are used on the same side of the straight letters as the circle, but in this style are little used. In some words, like *mostly, lastly*, the *t* is sacrificed by using the circle instead of the loop. Use the loop only as indicated in the exercises.

WRITING EXERCISE 13.

1. Use the *n*-hook in: Eden eaten sadden sudden bidden bitten button gotten kitten trodden maiden mutton mitten smitten laden leaden redden rotten wooden bounden even oven seven often soften proven graven striven leaven sloven raven riven orphan woven haven ashen heathen earthen lengthen strengthen omen common woman women earn born burn spurn turn torn acorn corn scorn fern shorn thorn morn mourn lorn horn. The alphabetic *En* is preferred in: Wagon reckon organ slacken liken ocean fusion allusion nutrition mission.

2. Use the *v*-hook in: Differ carve scarf curve serve surf observe subserve deserve turf reserve.

3. Use the shaded *Em* in: Pomp pump camp scamp damp tramp tramp stump stomp jump champ vamp mumps limp lamp lump rump romp enstamp, postage-stamp, but not in: pompous rumpus compass encompass impart import impair impossible impress impervious imperious impersonal imperfect impolite implead empower impanel empurple improper simple sample temple.

4. Use the shaded *Ar* in: Arch torch march urge merge surge search lurch charge George scourge starch porch barge, but not in: purge urchin margin origin original gorgeous courage courageous encourage.

5. Use the shaded *El* in: Pillar pallor tiller taller collar scholar valor cellar counselor chancellor Rensselaer insular.

14.

1. [shorthand content]

2. [shorthand content]

3. [shorthand content]

4. [shorthand content]

6. Use the shaded *Ra* in: Religion religious relict relinquish relevancy relish girl curl furl whirl whirl-wind marl pearl inaugural doggerel liberal chloral plural floral, but not in: relay rally early real relieve release relume relative relax reload.

7. Use the *Ste* loop in: Stub step steam stem stump stumble stir sterile store storage store-house storm starch start startle stark.

NOTE:—*Steer steerage* may be written in full, to distinguish them from *store* and *storage*; and so in other cases where necessary.

Use the *Est* loop in: Lapsed waxed vexed fixed mixed worst forced enforced burst endorsed discoursed first interest manifest alterest must most last least, at last, at least, utmost, uppermost foremost in the most mostly, most easily, most likely, lastly listless restless steamer steam pipe, steam engine, stimulus, storekeeper, story, storied, stepping stone, step-sister, step-mother.

WRITING EXERCISE 14.

1. Unfading hope! when life's last embers burn,
When soul to soul, and dust to dust return;
Heaven to thy charge resign the awful hour,
O! then, thy kingdom come, immortal power!

The sun with all its attendant planets is but a very little part of the grand machinery of the universe. Let us send light and joy, if we can, to every one around us. All great things are so only by the assemblage of small things. Keep an inventory of your friends rather than of your goods. Half of what passes among men for talent is nothing but good health.

2. By the faults and errors of others, wise men correct their own. Into every human being God has breathed an immortal soul.

Have respect for yourself that others may not disrespect you. We cannot turn in any direction where the Creator's love does not smile around us. A man may comfort himself for the wrinkles in his face provided his heart be fortified by virtue. If women fulfilled truly their divine errand there would be no need of societies for reform.

3. Men are never so easily deceived as when they plan to deceive others. A child in the humblest walks of life is as richly gifted as in the highest. Man gains wider dominion by his intellect than by his right arm. As the days begin to lengthen the cold begins to strengthen. Seven days make one week. He will learn to play the organ in the old oaken chapel on the hill. He often sought to soften the manners of the seven rude boys that formed his class.

4. Little by little the time goes by,
Short if you sing it, long if you sigh;
Little by little—an hour—a day;
Gone with the years that have vanished away.

We perceive the shadow to have moved along the dial, but did not see it moving; and it appears that the grass has grown, though nobody ever saw it grow; so the advances we make in knowledge, as they are made in minute steps, are perceivable only by the distance.

330 words to be written in 3¼ minutes and reduced to 2¼ minutes.

15.

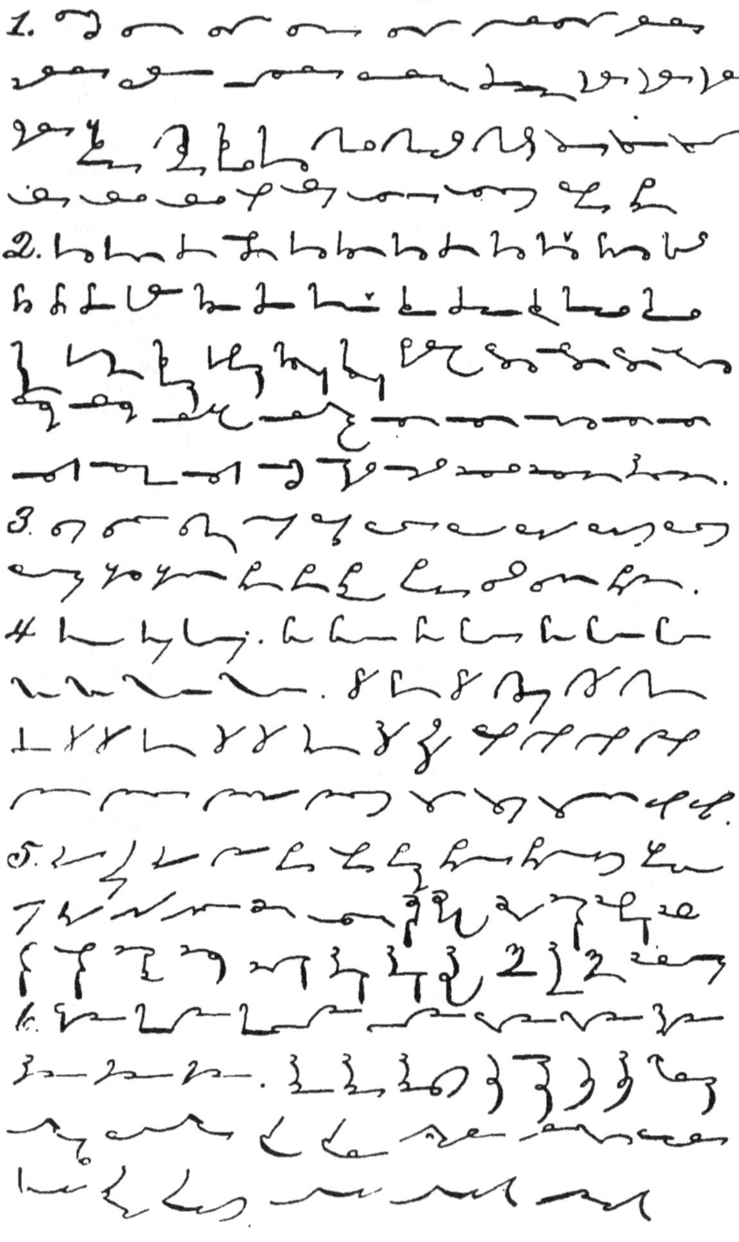

IN BUSINESS SHORTHAND. 65

WRITING EXERCISE 15. MISCELLANEOUS.

1. Sassafras sister system society schism monasticism rusticity elasticity solicitude domesticity statistical fastidious velocity felicity veracity sphericity absurdity imbecility precipitous preposterous impetus impetuous impulsive custody extrude extreme necessity necessities necessitous necessary ancestor ancestry ancestral sincerity serious.

2. Basis bases possess dispossess paces pieces praises passes process prices pleases palace police policy placid pellucid precede proceed preside passage postage paschal prodigious prejudice previous pervious prospective perspective prescribe proscribe superstition successes discusses classes encloses satisfied dissatisfied desolation dislocation decease disease diocese deceased diseased disrobe distribute disturb divers divorce diverse industries industrious illustrious.

3. Summer sumpter sympathy sooner scenery sentry center senator senatorial central sanitary arms armies serious series serene serenity sources sorrows ceremonious.

4. Binder bindery boundary plant planet pliant plenty blind blend blunt grind grand ground grunt blister bluster plaster embassador impostor imposture past pastor pastoral pester vaster faster fester investor Sylvester songster monster Munster Minster minister ministry ministerial minstrel custom customer extemporize wisdom western.

5. Literary literature literal mineral certain uncertain certify ceremony ceremoniously ascertain order reader writer rioter instruct uninstructed inseparable insupportable insecure insatiable insusceptible incessant sociable unsociable incipient incisive inestimable ineffaceable inevitable invisible invalid inveterate injurious incendiary.

6. Abominate predominate predeterminate terminate culminate criminate effeminate illuminate fulminate germinate infinite infinity infinitesimal offensive defensive offensively inoffensively inquisitive loquacious soliloquy require request requisite aristocracy generosity banquet liquid lingual languid languish relinquish.

WRITING EXERCISE 16.

1. To him, who, in the love of nature, holds
Communion with her visible forms, she speaks
A various language; for his gayer hours,
She has a voice of gladness, and a smile,
And eloquence of beauty; and she glides
Into his darker musing, with a mild,
And gentle sympathy, that steals away
Their sharpness, e'er he is aware.

2. Yet a few days, and thee,
The all beholding sun shall see no more
In all its course; nor yet in the cold ground,

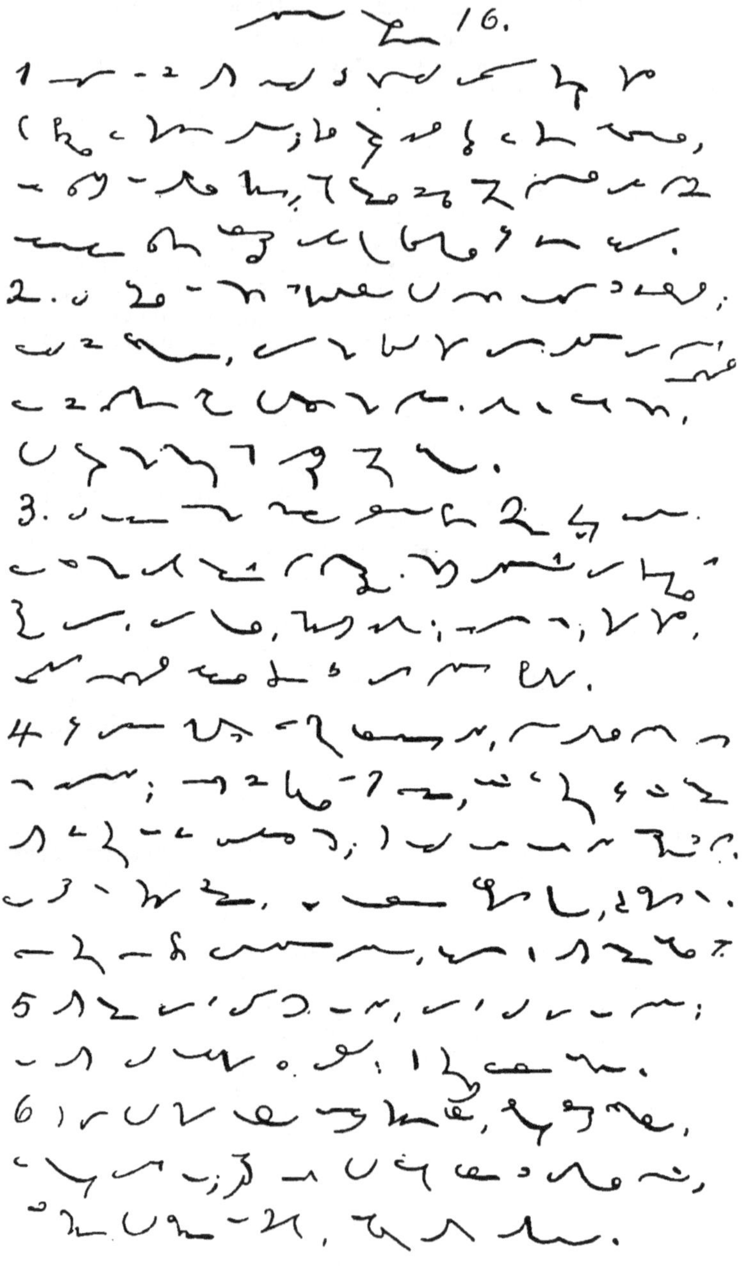
16.
1
2.
3.
4
5
6

Where thy pale form was laid, with many tears,
Nor in the embrace of ocean shall exist
Thy image. Earth, that nourish'd thee, shall claim
Thy growth, to be resolved to earth again.

3. Yet not to thy eternal resting place
Shal't thou retire alone—nor could'st thou wish
Couch more magnificent. Thou shalt lie down
With patriarchs of the infant world, with kings,
The powerful of the earth, the wise, the good,
Fair forms, and hoary seers of ages past,
All in one mighty sepulchre.

4. 'Ere wit oblique had broke that steady light,
Man, like his maker, saw that all was right;
To virtue, in the paths of pleasure trod,
And owned a father, when he owned a God.
Love, all the faith, and all the allegiance then,
For nature knew no right divine in men;
Nor ill could fear in God, and understood
A sovereign being, but a sovereign good.
True faith, true policy, united ran,
That was but love of God, and this of man.

5. Love God with all your soul and might,
With all your heart and mind;
And love your neighbor as yourself,
Be faithful, just, and kind.

6. For him, shall prayer unceasing and daily vows ascend;
His kingdom still increasing, a kingdom without end.
The heavenly dew shall nourish a seed in weakness sown,
Whose fruit shall spread and flourish, and shake like Lebanon.

311 words to be written in 3½ minutes and reduced to 2½ minutes.

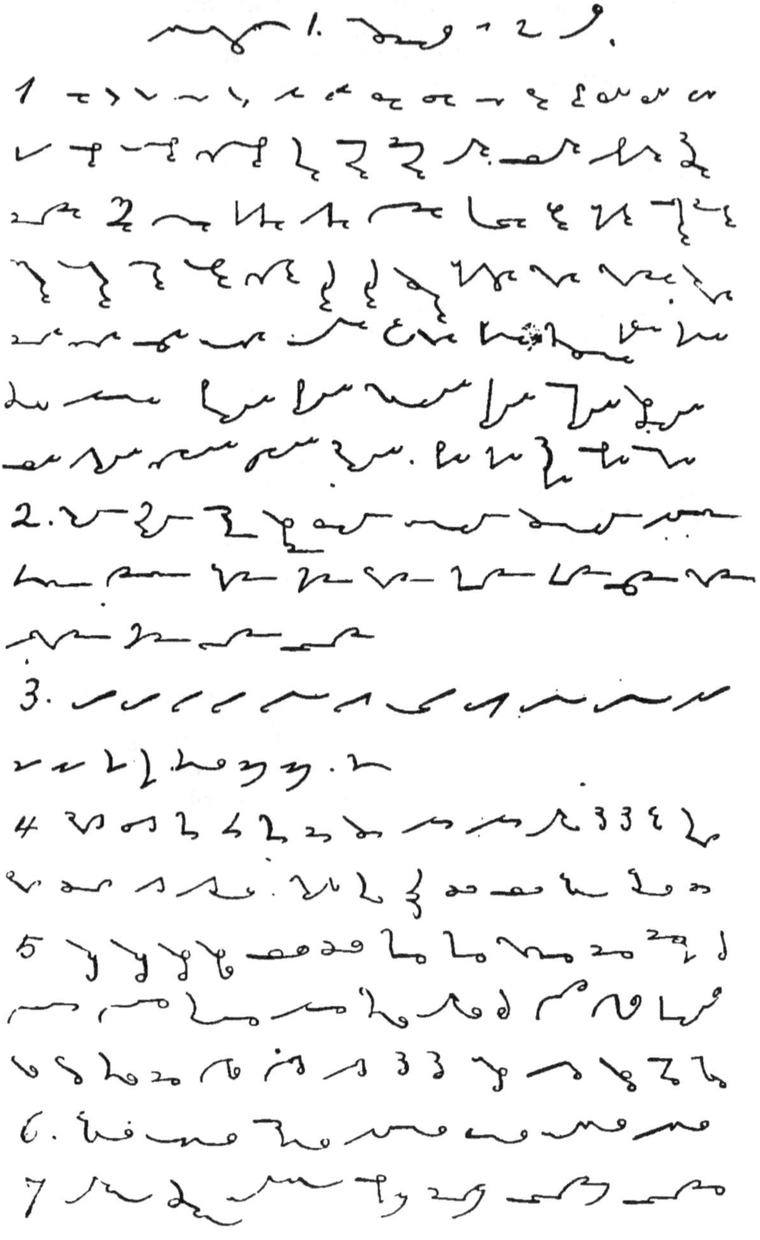
1.
2.
3.
4
5
6.
7

Chapter III.

Syllable Signs.—Prefixes and Affixes.

In Chapter II all the general principles of contraction in their original and more restricted sphere of use have been explained. In Chapter III, there is some extension of these principles, and the introduction of prefix and affix, or Syllable Signs.

Sec. 1. Extended Use of the Half Length Principle, and Signs for the Terminations, Ate, Ward, Ant, Ent, Bent, Dent, Ment, Ance and Ence.

1. The half length signs are always used where the vocal is excluded before the *d* and *t*; as taught in Chapter II. This principle is also applied to a few words of one syllable, in which a vowel occurs before the *d* or *t*. The list given in Chapter II, Sec. 8, Par. 6, may be extended somewhat; and the principle may be applied to such final syllables as *pate cate gate date tate shate mate nate late rate quate*; and in long words more freely.

2. The shortened form is not used when the vowel occurs before the final *ate*, nor in words in which it is more convenient to use an in-hook followed by a full length sign, as in *abominate*. The termination *vate* is written *Ve-Te* because the *a* cannot be conveniently joined to the *Ve*.

3. Where *rd* follows Wa and Ha the end of the stems of these letters is thickened to indicate it, as in the words, *word* and *hard*. This furnishes a proper sign for the termination *ward*, in *reward*.

4. The shortening principle applies also to syllables ending in the n-hook. And here the *d* or *t* is read after the hook. This furnishes signs for the syllables *bent dent tent vent tient cient ment rent* etc.

5. The n-hook is properly an in-hook, and the hook on the opposite side of the straight stems an an-hook. The circle added on the in-hook side gives the terminations *ins* and *ence*, and the circle in the an-hook the termination *ance*.

Writing Exercise 1.

Use shortened forms in the following words:

1. Date God guide sight thought rate hate state straight tight skate plate slate slight white better; and in the final syllables of dissipate anticipate emancipate vacate delicate indelicate locate dislocate reciprocate investigate intimidate invalidate sedate perpetrate arbitrate meditate penetrate associate appreciate depreciate initiate ingratiate negotiate satiate insatiate emaciate vitiate officiate excruciate approximate cremate criminate acclimate intimate estimate decimate animate alternate amalgamate subordinate procrastinate personate fortunate fascinate originate speculate stipulate granulate populate depopulate expostulate desolate regulate emulate stimulate inoculate separate operate evaporate desperate decorate

2. Use full length forms in. graduate fluctuate deviate expiate situate attenuate extenuate radiate roseate mediate abominate

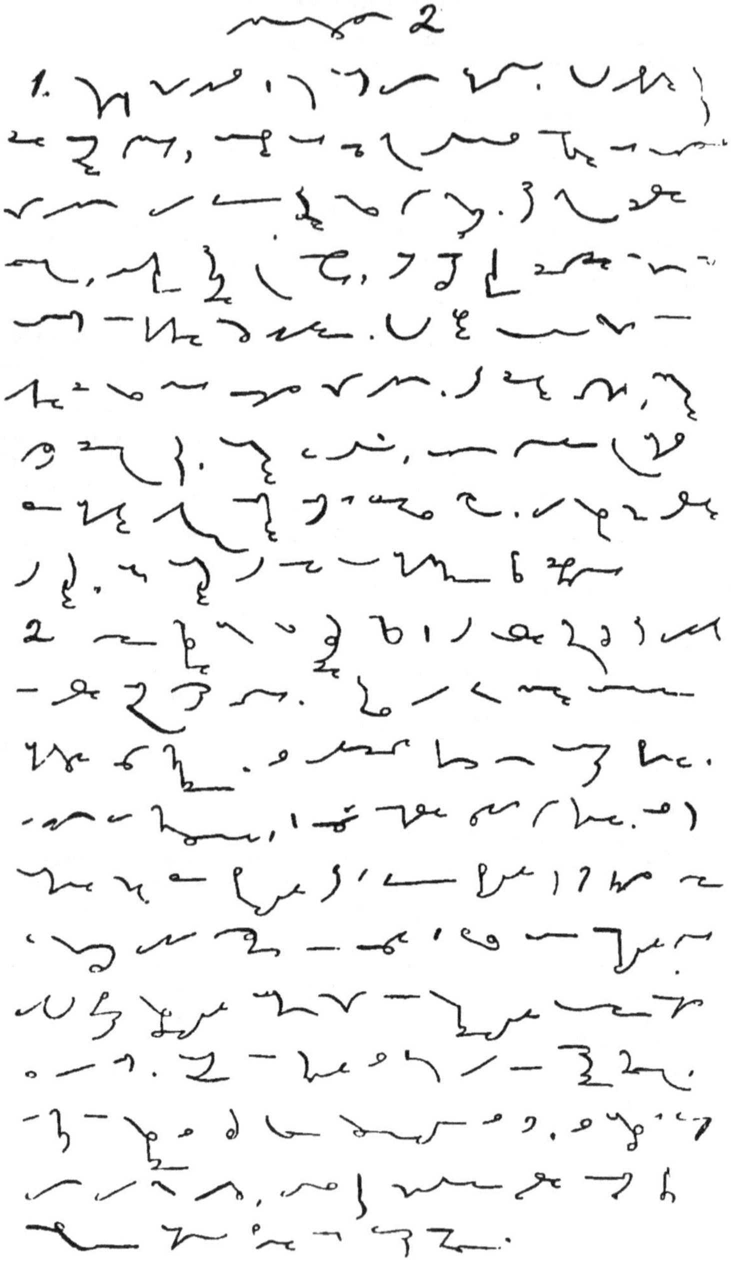

IN BUSINESS SHORTHAND. 71

germinate culminate predominate ruminate disseminate criminate recriminate fulminate terminate determinate.

3. Word ward heard hard harden hardy unheard warder warden wording reward.

Word-signs: Inward outward forward afterward forwardness inwardly outwardly virtuous.

4. Incumbent, serpent prudent ardent verdant intent extent regent urgent eloquent invent infant ancient figment segment instrument repent repentance occupant vacant elephant instant distant abandon abundance incident.

5. Cabin cabins expense expanse distance instant prudence pretence credence intense intensify pence mountain mountains fountains regions fragrance eloquence fence immense ambulance petulance glance glens vagrants intents implants imprints reprints invents infants acceptance reluctance exactness directness compactness.

6. Abeyance annoyance defiance radiance audience alliance reliance.

7. Locating investigating alternating desperately intimately determinateness.

WRITING EXERCISE, 2.

1. There may have been greater writers but there never was a better man. They will reciprocate the favor in a delicate manner, and dissipate any doubts of their willingness to placate any animosities that may arise. We ought to investigate the case more carefully. If he can elucidate the truth he will be able to invalidate their testimony, and will doubtless be able to intimidate those who have endeavored to perpetrate this outrage. They will associate under an agreement to arbitrate in the case of any difference that may arise. He will initiate the movement, ingratiate himself into their favor, negotiate a loan, and so manage their affairs as to appreciate rather than to depreciate the value of the stocks in question. We expect that the licentiate will officiate, and that the novitiate will take an appropriate place in the ceremony.

2. Such precipitate action cannot facilitate the business, but will necessitate further efforts if we wish to resuscitate the flagging zeal of many. The funds are altogether inadequate and do not approximate the sum appropriated. His legitimate position is entirely subordinate. He always would procrastinate, but desired to personate some one more fortunate. It is very unfortunate that he should still speculate while he ought to stipulate for sure returns. Such a causeless war is certain to decimate all sections, and to depopulate many. We shall certainly expostulate, and advise them to capitulate on such terms as are offered. Unwilling to violate his oath, or to deviate from the truth, he preferred to expiate his offence than to extenuate his fault. His acceptance of the charge was with great reluctance, yet it is believed that he will not hesitate to follow the policy designated, and remain subordinate to the chief director.

295 words to be written in 3 minutes and reduced to 2¼ minutes.

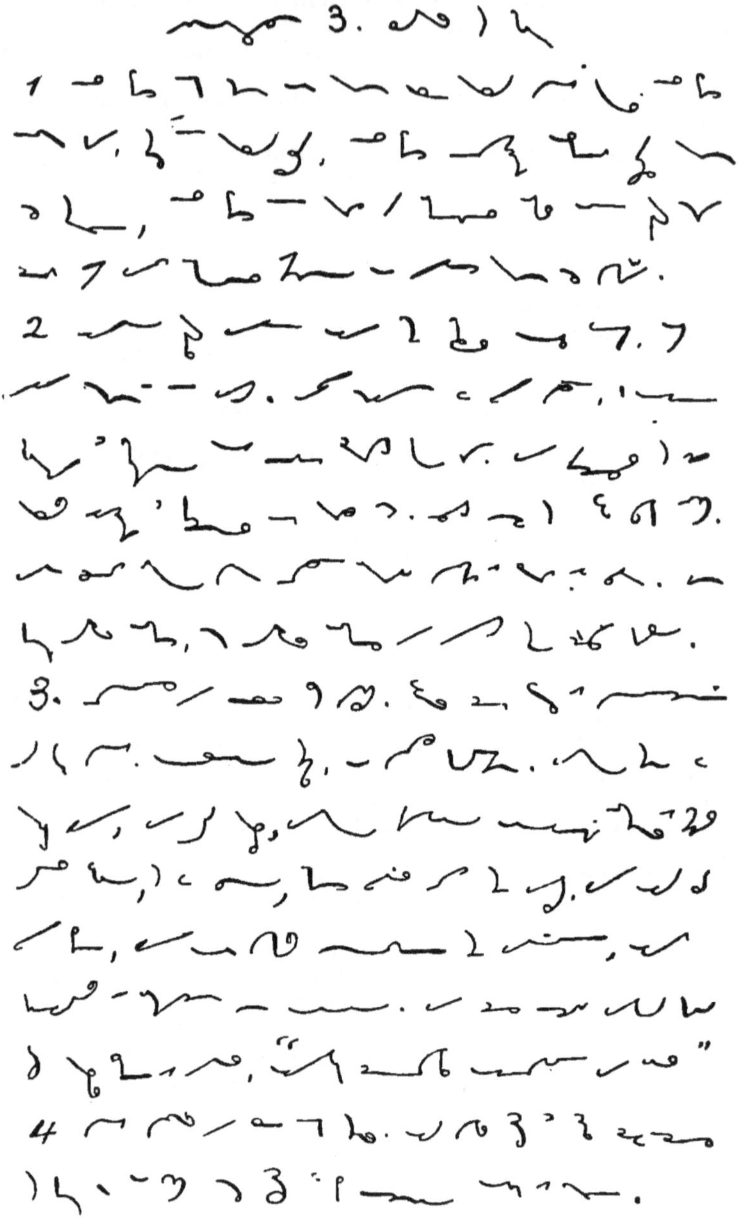

IN BUSINESS SHORTHAND. 73

Writing Exercise 3.

1. It is pleasant to be virtuous and good, because that is to excel many others; it is pleasant to grow better, because that is to excel ourselves; it is pleasant to mortify and subdue our lusts, because that is victory; it is pleasant to command our appetites and passions, and to keep them in due order within the bounds of reason and religion, because that is empire.

2. The warden keeps watch and ward over the prisoners under his charge, and will reward those who do well. We heard that he was a hard master, but not backward in performing any duty incumbent upon him. With ardent desire for inward excelence, he went forward in obedience to the commands of God. A serpent is a very ancient symbol of evil. With that instrument he can make the most accurate measurement of the segment of a circle. He is both eloquent and prudent; though eloquence and prudence are rarely found in the same person.

3. The mountains are distant several miles. A glance into the glens of the mountain side will show many interesting fissures, and immense boulders. We can find a cabin, where with little expense we can remain, and enjoy the fragrance of the flowers. Let us abandon for a season the busy haunts of man for the wilderness, were nature holds her sceptre, where no ambulance is needed for the wounded, and where the petulance of avarice is unknown. With intense delight we shall behold the vast expanse spread out around us, and "worship in the temple not made with hands."

4. Many immigrants are said to be vagrants. Nature implants, even in infants, innate tendencies for both good and evil: this evinces a special design on the part of the Creator.

300 words to be written in 3 minutes and reduced to 2¼.

Sec. 2. The Terminations Zhn Shn Zhnl Shnl.

The terminations *sion tion cian sian tian* etc., pronounced *zhn* and *shn* are treated as follows:

1. Omit *shn* after an added vocal.
2. Write Zhe for *zhn*, with or without a vocal.
3. On Be Pe Ka Ve Ef and Ar, where no vocal occurs before *shn*, use a large right-hand hook: this kook is also used on De Te with an omitted Ka, and on Ef for *ficution and faction*.
4. After the n-hook, a second hook may be added for *shn*, where it follows En without a vocal.
5. *Ish-La,* or *Shcl*, may be written for *shnl*; and *Ish-La-Te,* or *Shcl-Te* for *shnlty.*
6. *Uation* and *ulation* are written with a large hook on Ya and Yater.

See corresponding numbers in Writing Exercise 4.

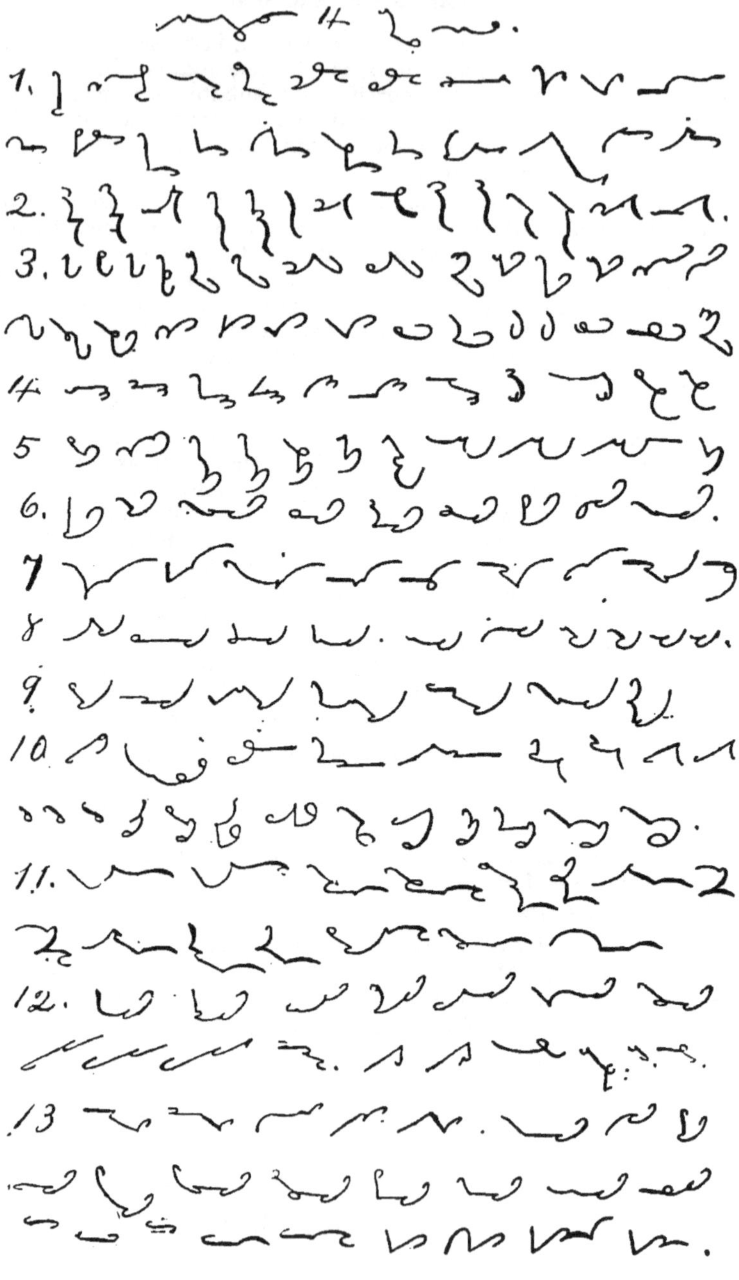

Sec. 8· The Terminations Meter, Liter, Ure, Urally, Ual, Ually, Ular, Ularly, Tude, Ize, Ness, Less and With.

1. Lengthened Em and El provide signs for the affixes *meter* and *liter*.
2. Ya is written for *ure* with an enlarged hook for *ual* and *ural* and with an added tick for a final *y*.
3. Ya is lengthened for *ular* and El is added for *ly*.
4. Te-De is written for *tude*, Sle for *self*, Ish for *ship*, and a circle only is sometimes added for *ness*.
5. Ze is written for *ize*, and Za for *ization*.

Sec. 4. The Terminations Ian Ien Iar Ier Ior with I coalescent.

1. Ian and ion are written with the yen-hook, *iar ier* and *ior* are treated like *ure*.
2. Ya may be sometimes omitted before the termination *ment*, and El before the termination *ion*.

Sec. 5. The Terminations Ed and Ing.

The termination *ed* may be indicated by the short vocal *e* at the end of a word where the De cannot be added; and the termination Ing may be added by a slanting tick; but De and Ing are to be preferred where the letters can be used conveniently.

Writing Exercise 4. Affix Signs.

1. Probation emancipation negation suffocation elucidation solicitation institution promotion commotion diminution edition, superstition proposition position imposition exposition physician amunition recognition magician logician.
2. Infusion effusion allusion provision prevision vision elision decision evasion invasion corrosion explosion erosion adhesion.
3. Objection subjection option perception affection protection election selection inflection apportion proportion aversion emersion immersion impression expression expulsion emission remission omission commision sanction function faction fiction ascension dissension infliction.
4. Attention intention pretention retention mention dimension declension invention intervention succession accession.
5. Sectional emotional provisional professional exceptional optional occasional.
6. Population graduation gratulation situation infatuation insinuation stipulation stimulation granulation.
7. Thermometer barometer chronometer diameter decimeter decameter millimeter decaliter deciliter.
8. Lecture stature posture panier annual manual actual gradual natural naturally.
9. Secular titular oracular vernacular jocular granular valvular.
10. Herself, their own self, solicitude fortitude rectitude partnership ownership hardship worship goodness greatness gladness wilfulness skillfulness helplessness sleeplessness graciousness wilderness fretfulness fruitfulness gracefulness gracelessness.

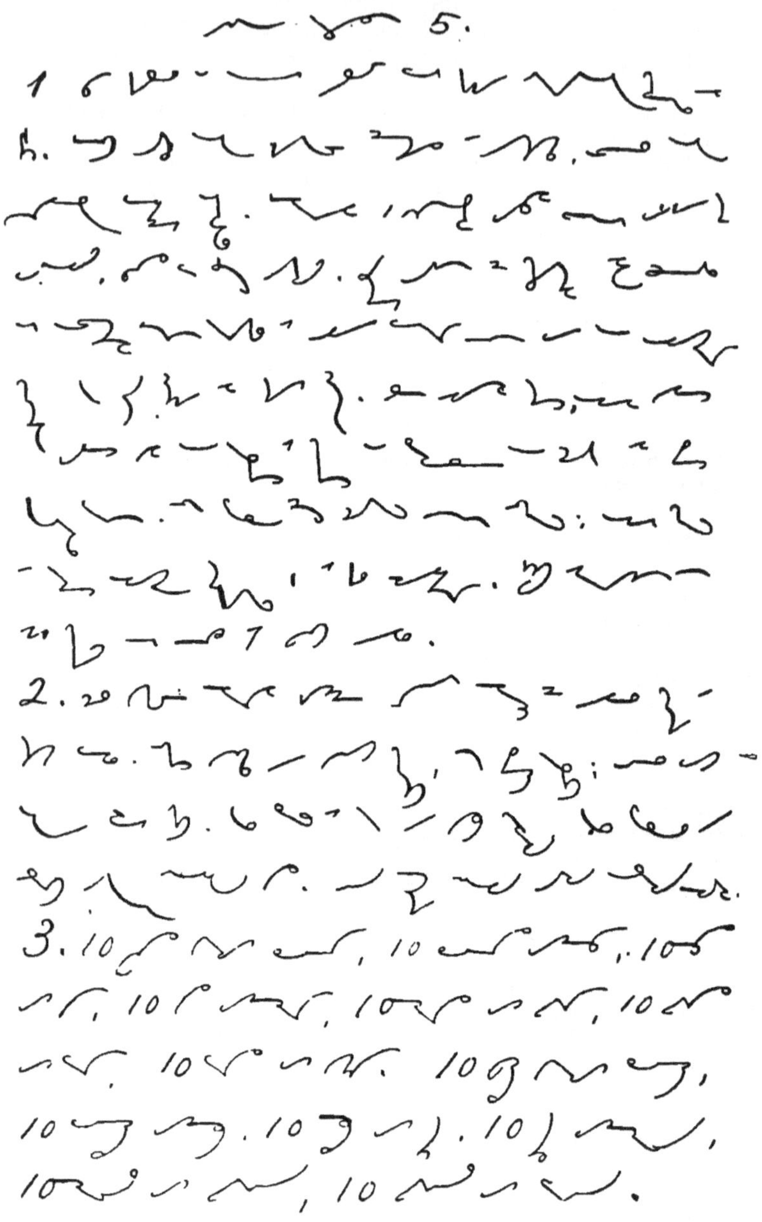

11. Colonize colonization crystallize crystallization sacrifice philosophize legalize civilize civilization localize vocalize vulgarize secularization christianize Methodize.

12. Bunion pinion alien civilian union communion christian herewith wherewith wherewithal indicated repented repenting intersecting accepting accounted discounted.

13. Document integument monument ornament argument cotillion million billion trillion quadrillion quintillion sextillion septillion octillion nonillion decillion gentlemen gentleman children generalize generalization perfection imperfection perfectionism perfectionist.

Writing Exercise 5.

1. Some persons have neither the resolution nor the power of carrying their projects to a completion. The devil loves nothing better than the intolerance of reformers, and dreads nothing so much as their charity and patience. The Declaration of Emancipation was made during the war for the Union, sometimes called the Southern Rebellion. Our safety lies in the preservation of American Institutions, and the neutralization of those corruptions of the old world which come to us with an unwelcome profusion. They live in fear of a foreign invasion. He said he was a physician, and not a magician. The logician made an exposition of the proposition, and suggested an elision of a certain obnoxious clause. The great question in this election is that of protection: not the protection of cotton and woolen fabrics, but of the boys who wear them. The inflation of the currency is out of all proportion to the demands of our commercial relations.

2. In his impassioned declamation, he mentioned the marked declension in the religious fervor of former generations. The present measures are merely provisional, though certainly exceptional, and it is well that they are only optional. These sections of the country are mostly agricultural. These questions are of sectional, rather than of national importance. He will deliver the annual lecture on secular education.

3. Ten millimeters make one centimeter, ten centimeters one decimeter, ten decimeters one meter, ten meters one decameter, ten decameters one hectometer, ten hectometers one kilometer, ten kilometers one myrameter.

Ten milliliters make one centiliter, ten centiliters one deciliter, ten deciliters one liter, ten liters one decaliter, ten decaliters one hectoliter, ten hectoliters one kiloliter.

273 words to be written in 3 minutes and reduced to 2 minutes.

Writing Exercise 6.

The North American Indian.—*Sprague.*

1. Not many generations ago, where we now sit, encircled with all that exalts and embellishes civilized life, the rank thistle nodded in the wind, and the wild fox dug his hole unscared. Here lived and

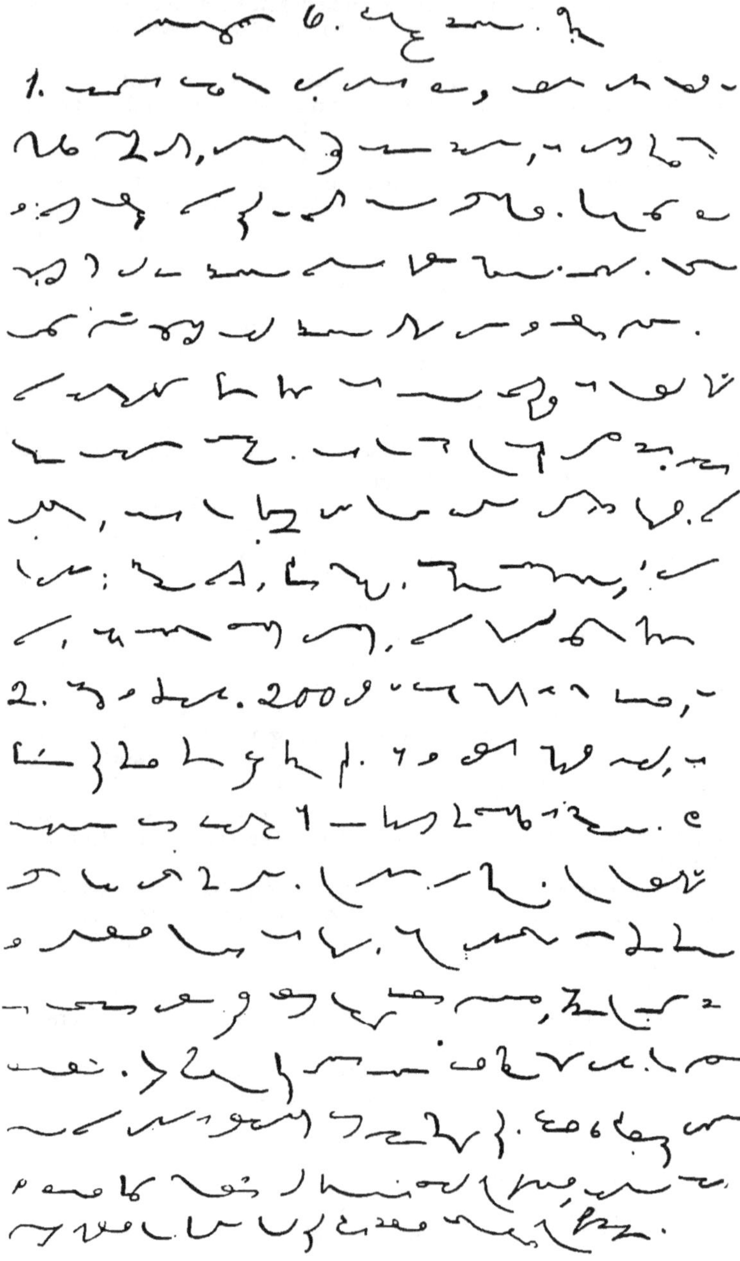

loved another race of beings. Beneath the same sun that rolls over your heads, the Indian hunter pursued the panting deer. Gazing on the same moon that smiles on you, the Indian lover wooed his dusky mate. Here the wigwam blaze beamed on the tender and helpless, and the council fire glowed on the wise and daring. Now they dip their noble limbs into the sedgy lake, and now they paddle the light canoe along your rocky shores. Here they warred: the echoing whoop, the bloody grapple, the defying death song, all were here; and when the tiger strife was over, here curled the smoke of peace.

2. And all this has passed away. Two hundred years has changed the character of a great continent, and blotted forever from its face a whole peculiar people. Art has usurped the bowers of nature, and the anointed children of education have been too powerful for the tribes of the ignorant. As a race they have withered from the land, their arrows are broken, their council fire has long since gone out on the shore. and their war cry is fast fading to the untrodden west. Slowly and sadly they climb the distant mountains, and read their doom in the setting sun. They are shrinking before the mighty tide which is pressing them away. They must soon hear the roar of the last wave which will settle over them forever. Ages hence the inquisitive white man as he stands by some growing city will ponder on the structure of their remains, and wonder to what manner of persons they belonged. They will live only in the songs and chronicles of their exterminators.

310 words to be written in 3¼ minutes and reduced to 2¼ minutes.

SEC. 6. CONTRACTED PREFIX SIGNS.

1. The prefix *ad* omits De before Ve and Ja.

2. The prefixes *Com* and *Con* are written by a tick joined to the straight signs when unmodified, and in the same direction with them when initial hooks and circles occur; and in the same direction with curved signs in all cases.

3. The tick for *Com* occurs only before the letters Be and Pe and the prefix *Con* before all the consonants except Be Pe Em Wa Ya and Ha. This prefix sign occurs after other prefixes in which case it is sometimes ommitted.

4. *Contra-tre-tri* and *Counter* add a final hook to the tick.

5. *Intra-tre-tri* and *-tro* omit the Ar, and *trance* omits the n and r.

6. *Stra* is written for *extra*, and an initial loop on Em Ra and Ar for *extem* and *exter*. This loop is enlarged on Em in *extreme* and its derivatives. The prefix *ex* loses the circle before the initial Pla, as in *explore*.

7. Ma is written for the prefix *im*, but the prefix *em* is vocalized. Where the prefix *in* cannot be joined, *en* is sometimes substituted for it.

8. When the prefixes *Pre* and *Pro* occur before Ve and Ef, they may be written with a large initial hook on these letters.

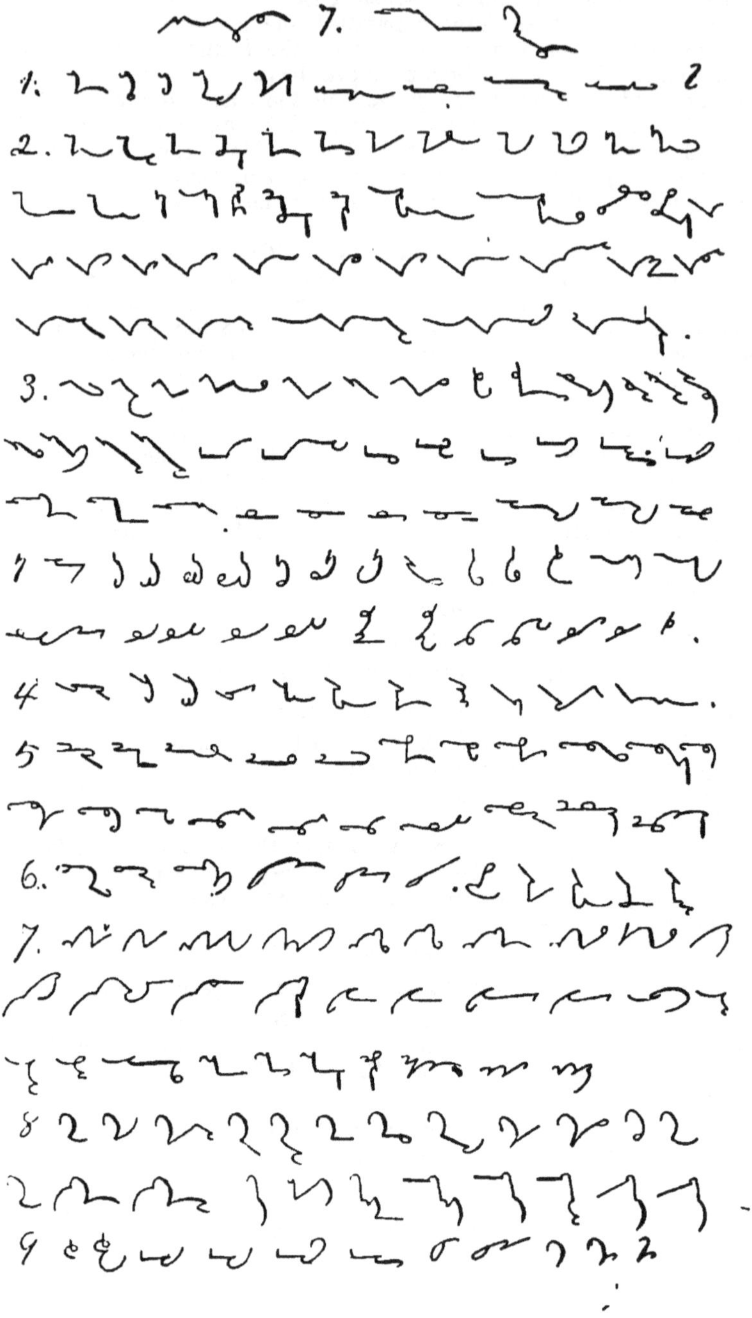

WRITING EXERCISE 7. CONTRACTED PREFIXES.

1. Advise advance advent adventure adverb adjoin adjust adjudicate Adjutant adjourn.

2. Combine combination combat combustible compose composition compare comparison compel compulsion comprehend comprehension compound component cumber encumber incomplete incombustible incompatible uncomplaining noncompliance circumstance circumscribe commit commute commission command commandment commend commence common commune commemorate commensurate commiserate commingle comic communicate intercommunication intercommunion incommunicable.

3. Connection concussion concord concordance concur conquer concurrence conception conspiracy consecutive consecrate consecration conclusive Congress congressional congregate congregation condemn condemnation condense condensation condition conditional contagion contortion controversy contribute contract concede consider constant construe conjecture conjectural congestion conjure conjure convene convention conventions convenience converse convulse convulsion conquest conscious conscience concession connive connubial consanguinity consult consultation console consolation conciliate conciliation consume consummation concern concert consort.

4. Contradict contravene contravention contrary contraband counterpane counterpoise counterfeit counterpart counterwork countersign.

5. Intrigue intrepid intrinsic introduce introduction transpose transplant transparent transpress transcribe transfer transform transverse transient transmigrate transmute transmit translate Trans-Atlantic intransitive intransmissible.

6. Extravagant extricate extra-professional extemporize extremity exterior external explore explain explicit explicate.

7. Empire impair impurple imperil empress impress embrace imburse reimburse material immaterial immaculate immodest immeasurable mortal immortal mortality immortality indwell initiate initiation insatiate injudicious inhabit inhabitant inhabitable inhospitable inharmonious inherent inherently.

8. Prevent prevail prevaricate provoke provocation provide providence prefigure prefer preference profess profane profound improvise improvisation prove approve private deprive deprave depreciate reprove reproof.

9. Conversation conversational continue continual continuation contingent extreme extraordinary improve improvement adjournment.

WRITING EXERCISE 8. SELECTIONS FOR PRACTICE.

1. Before they adjourn the meeting, they will adjust the matter according to the decision of the adjutant. Though a noncombatant in principle, he approved very highly of the measures for strengthen-

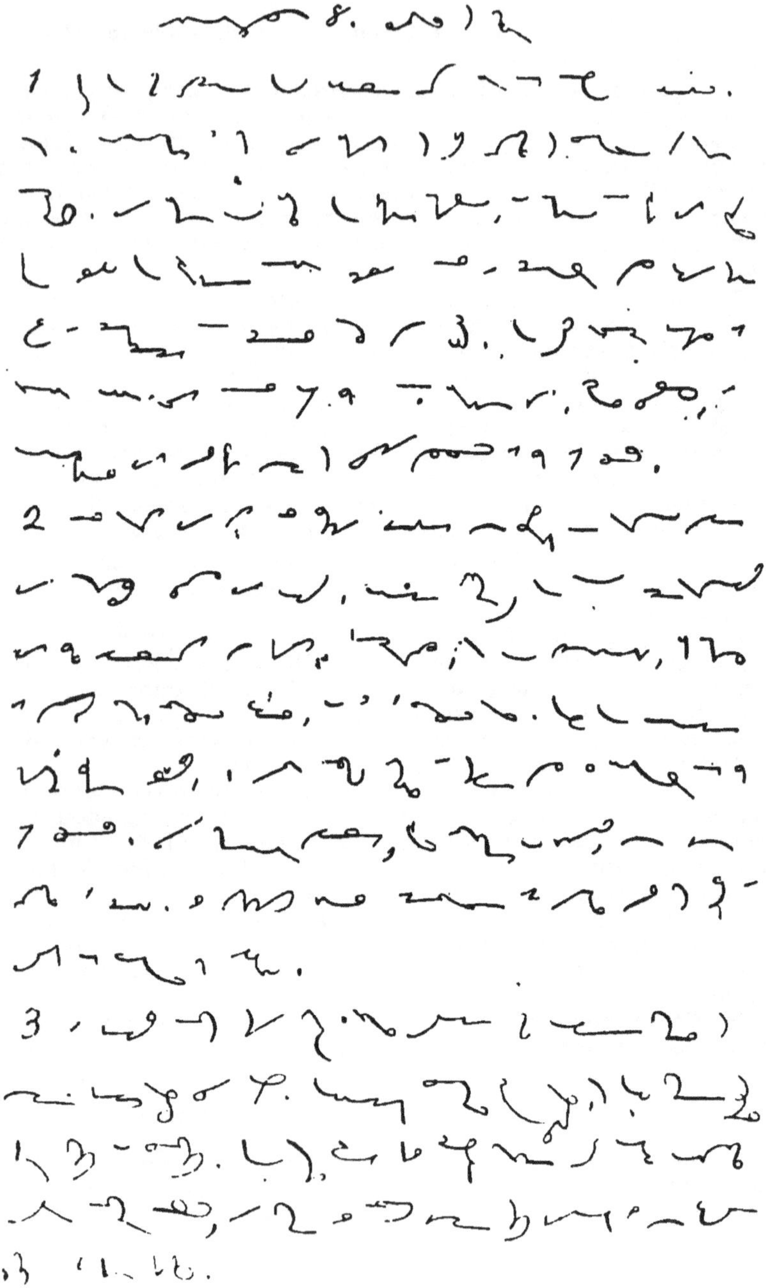

ing our coast defences. We advise an advance. They comprehend the comparison, and combine to comply with the request. Upon consultation, they concluded to act in concert. It is of intrinsic importance that we find a man of intrepidity to introduce this important invention. They flatly contradict the terms of the contract, and act contrary to its entire spirit. To accuse him in these circumstances of noncompliance with the rules of the establishment, is a very extraordinary misconstruction of the spirit of our instructions.

2. It is common with men, whose sphere of duty is circumscribed, to commune much with themselves, sometimes with nature, and not infrequently they enter into communion with the spirits of just men made perfect. The Ten Commandments, given on Mount Sinai, have been the basis of all moral law throughout the Christian ages, and in all Christian countries. They say they do not approve the conspiracy of silence, but regard the suppression of facts of vital importance as antagonistic to the spirit of our institutions. Her Britannic Majesty, the Queen of Great Britian and Ireland, is also Empress of India. His Imperial Highness, the Autocrat of all the Russias, rules over a large part of Europe and the northern part of Asia.

3. He continues to improve every occasion. Congress will not adjourn until it provides for such contingent expenses as are necessary. They have not been extravagant in their expenditures though they have provided facilities both professional and extra-professional. Being governed only by his insatiable greed. he will initiate no measures likely to provoke dissension, or prevent his control of such official patronage as he is able to pervert to his base purposes.

310 words to be written in 3 minutes and reduced to 2¼ minutes.

WRITING EXERCISE 9. THE DISCOVERY OF AMERICA.—*Everett*,

1. The discovery itself of the American Continent may, I think, fairly be considered the most extraordinary event in the history of the world. In this, as in other cases, familiarity blunts the edge of our perceptions. But much as I have meditated, and often as I have treated this theme, its magnitude grows upon me, with each successive contemplation. That a continent nearly as large as Europe and Africa united, spread out on both sides of the Equator, lying between the western shores of Europe and Africa and the eastern shore of Asia, with groups of islands in either ocean, as it were stepping places on the march of discovery, a continent, not inhabited indeed by civilized races, but, still, occupied by one of the families of rational men, that this great hemisphere, I say, should have lain undiscovered for 5000 years upon the bosom of the deep, a mystery so vast within so short a distance, and yet not found out, is indeed a marvel.

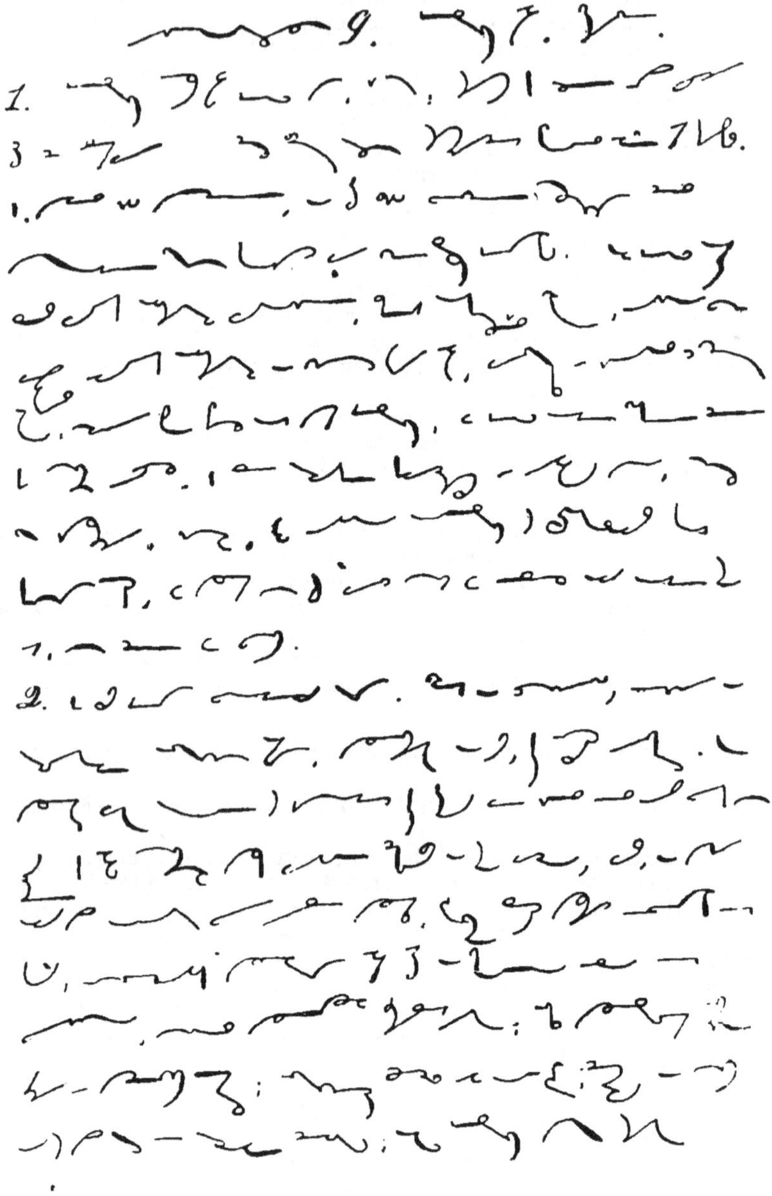

2. But the fulness of time had not yet come. Egypt and Assyria, and Tyre, and Carthage, and Greece, and Rome, must flourish and fall before the seals are broken. They must show what they can do for humanity, before the vail which hides its last hope is lifted up. The ancient civilization must be weighed in the balance, and found wanting. Yes, and more. Nature must unlock her rarest mysteries; the quivering steel must learn to tremble to the pole; the Astrolabe must climb the arch of heaven, and bring down the sun to the horizon; science must demonstrate the sphericity of the earth: the press must scatter the flying rear of mediaeval darkness; the creative instincts of a new political, intellectual and social life must begin to kindle into action; and then the discovery may go forth.

300 words to be written in 3 minutes and reduced to 2 minutes.

SECTION 7. CONTRACTED PHRASES, AND WORD OMISSIONS.

1. In forming Phrase Signs the words *a*, *and*, *from*, *of*, *the*, *of the* and *to*, are sometimes omitted.

2. In places where they can be easily inferred, as in the opening of a letter, other words are sometimes omitted, as "*your's received*," for "*your favor received.*"

3. In some cases the omitted word may be indicated by proximity, (the writing of the words closer together than is usual;) or by intersection, (the striking of a letter through a preceding one.)
These methods of contraction should be used sparingly.

SEC. 8. PUNCTUATION IN NOTE TAKING.

Only two marks of punctuation are essential, but these should not be omitted. The Period and Interrogation should always be indicated. The Period may be indicated by a space of about an inch in length; and the mark of Interrogation may be written without the dot.

WRITING EXERCISE 10.

1. Time of the year, day of the week, nations of the earth, laws of the land, wealth of the nation, the rules of the art, history of the world, inspiration of the bible, importance of the measure, one of the family, waves of the ocean, sands of the desert, stars of the sky, close of the year, close of the day, the value of the consignment.

2. From time to time, from place to place, from side to side, from day to day, from hour to hour, from week to week, from month to month, from generation to generation.

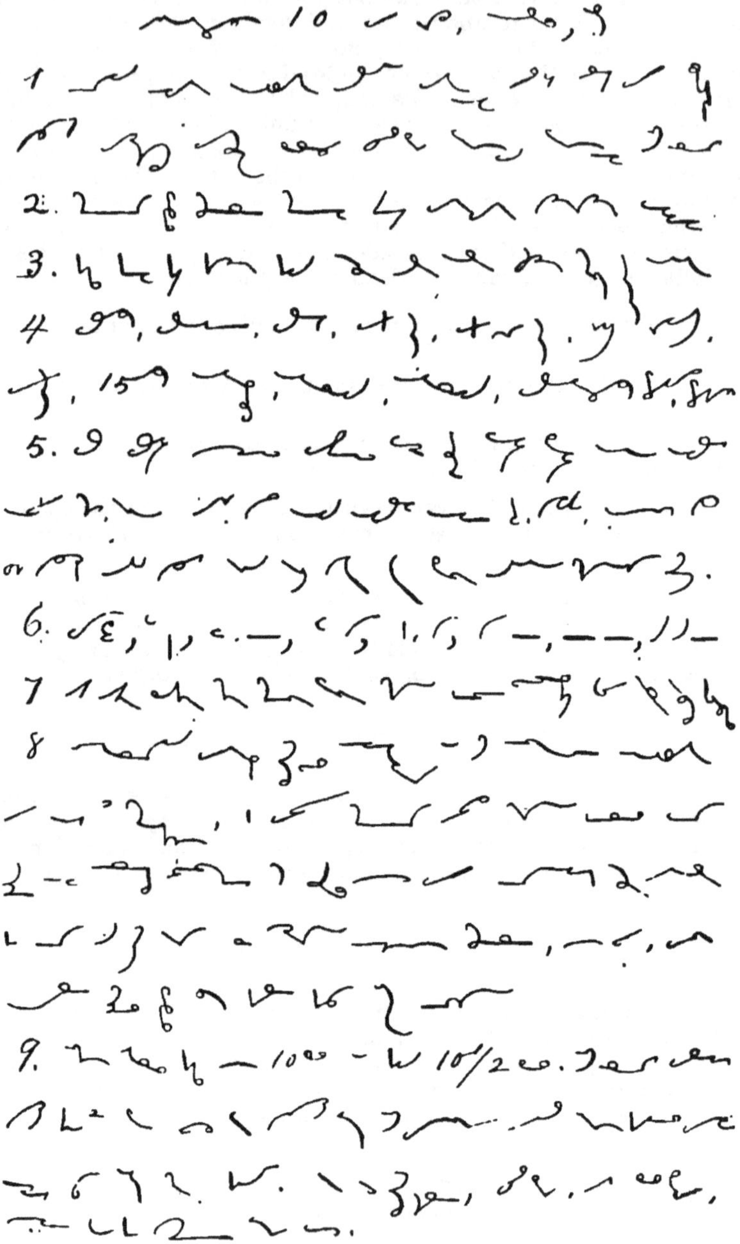

3. By the piece, by the day, by the hour, by the month, by the year, this week, last week, next week, last month, over and over forever and ever, now and then.

4. Your favor received, your favor received and contents noted, your esteemed favor received, we beg to acknowledge the receipt of your favor, we beg to acknowledge the receipt of your esteemed favor, I have received your letter, I am in receipt of your letter, we are in receipt of your favor, your favor of the 15th inst. is received, enclosed please find, enclosed we (I) hand you, enclosed we (I) send you, your's with enclosures received, please reply at once, please reply by return mail.

5. United States, United States of America, Eastern Continent, Western Continent, Atlantic Ocean, Pacific Ocean, North America, South America, New England, New York City, New Hampshire, Vermont, Connecticut, Rhode Island, Massachusettes, New York, New York State, New Jersey, Pennsylvania, Maryland, North Carolina, Mississippi, Louisiana, Missouri, Colorado, California, Michigan, Chicago, South Carolina, London, Birmingham, Philadelphia.

6. Y. M. C. A., A. B., A. D., A. M., P. M., M. D., D. D., L. L. D.

7. Railroad, railroad car, sleeping car, parlor car, freight car, coal car, brakeman, conductor, train despatcher, engineer, express company, express office, baggage express.

8. At this time of the year we expect the leaves of the trees to change color and fall to the ground.

The nations of the earth are now in profound peace; but we hear from time to time rumors of coming contests, which may lead to a disturbance of the tranquility over large sections of the eastern world. It may not be this week, or next week, but the time will surely come, As a sick man tosses from side to side, so he, with great unrest, flits from place to place, as though pursued by some avenging demon.

·9. The price of those goods by the piece is 10 cents, and by the yard $10\frac{1}{2}$ cents.

The value of the consignment was not the material point in the question, it was altogether immaterial whether the value was greater or less. The cost of the purchase was a definite sum, and should be protected by law.

Go count the leaves of the forest, the stars of the sky, or the sands of the sea-shore,—such shall be the multitude of thy children.

480 words to be written in $4\frac{1}{2}$ minutes, and reduced to 3 minutes.

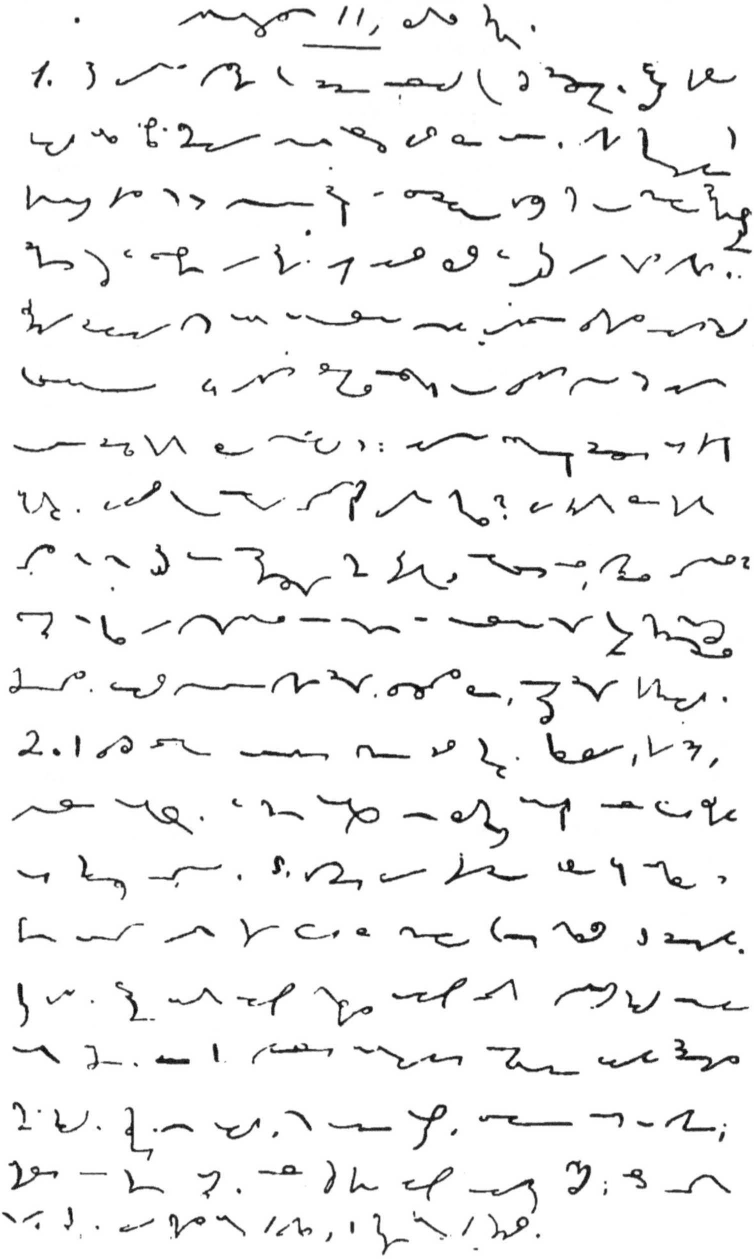

Writing Exercise 11.

1. If we are not misinformed, they intend to discontinue their efforts in this direction. A thoughtless person continually acts and speaks as if it were no consequence what is said and done. Robert Breckenridge very pertinently remarks, that God is not incapable of extricating himself from an eternal incomprehensibility. In composition, there is a transposed, or inverted order of words, as well as a conventional, or common arrangement. The sphere in which we move, and act, and understand, is of a wider circumference to one creature than to another. When the Roman historians described an extraordinary man, this always entered into his character as an essential of it: He was of incredible industry, and remarkable application.

What words can declare the immeasurable worth of books? What rhetoric set forth the importance of that great invention which diffuses them over the whole earth, to gladden its myriads of minds? Truly good books are more than mines to those who understand them. They are the breathings of the great souls of past times. Genius is not embalmed in them, as is sometimes said, but lives in them perpetually.

2. Be servants of truth and duty, each in his vocation. Be sincere, pure in heart, earnest, enthusiastic. A virtuous enthusiasm is self-forgetful and noble. It is the only inspiration now vouchsafed to man. Blend humility with learning. Ascend above the present in place and time. Regard fame only as the eternal shadow of excellence. Bend in adoration before the right. Cultivate alike the wisdom of experience and the wisdom of hope. Mindful of the future, do not neglect the past; awed by the majesty of antiquity, turn not away in indifference from the future.

Prosperity is naturally, though not necessarily, attached to virtue and merit; adversity to vice and folly. It is the first point of wisdom to ward off evils, the second to make them beneficial. We promise according to our hopes, but perform according to our fears.

326 words to be written in 3 minutes and reduced to 2¼ minutes.

Writing Exercise 12.—Selections for Practice.

1. The only distinctions which should be recognized in society, are those of the soul of the intellect and of the heart—of a soul strong in principle, incorruptible in integrity; of an intellect cultivated and true, ready to accept, and strong to defend the truth; of a heart filled with love to God and man. That fortitude which has encountered no dangers, that prudence which has surmounted no difficulties, that integrity which has been attended by no temptations, can at best be considered but as gold not yet brought to the test.—*Channing.*

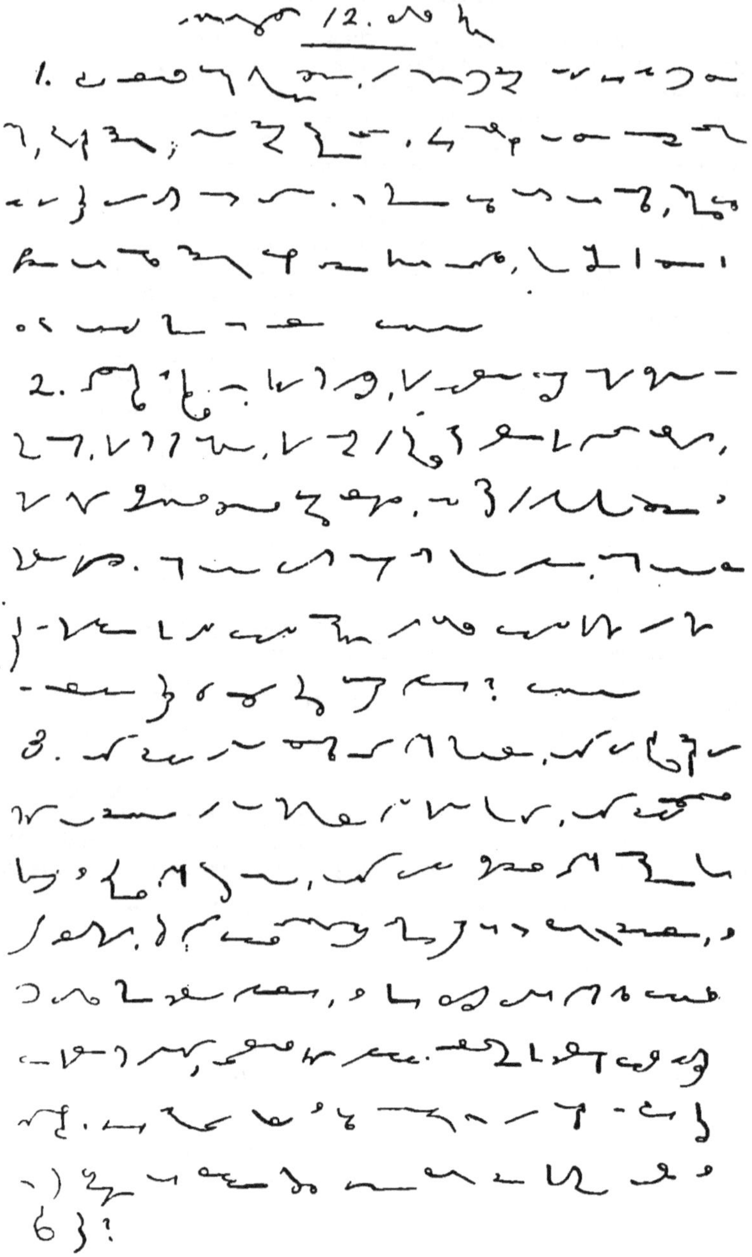

IN BUSINESS SHORTHAND. 91

2. The most precious of all possessions is power over ourselves; power to withstand trials, to bear suffering, to front danger, power over pleasure and pain; power to follow our convictions, however resisted by menace and scorn; the power of calm self-reliance in seasons of darkness and storms; to have even our earthly being extended in everlasting remembrance; to be known wherever the name of virtue can reach; and to be known as the benefactor of every age, by the light which we have difused, or the actions which we have performed or prompted—who does not feel some desire for this additional immortality?

3. No matter in what language the strangers doom may have been pronounced; no matter what complexion incompataole with freedom an Indian or an African sun may have burned upon him; no matter in what disastrous battle his liberties may have been cloven down, no matter with what solemnities he may have been devoted upon the altar of slavery; the first moment he touches the sacred soil of Britain, the altar and the God sink together into the dust; his soul walks abroad in her own majesty; his body swells beyond the measure of his chains that burst from around him; and he stands redeemed, regenerated, disenthralled by the irresistible Genius of Universal Emancipation.

How can he exalt his thoughts to anything great or noble, who only believes that after a short term, he is to sink into oblivion, and lose his conciousness forever.

343 words to be written in 3½ minutes and reduced to 2¼.

WRITING EXERCISE 13.

Extract from Lecture by Edward Everett.

1. The modern temperance agitation commenced more than seventy five years ago. The subject has been before the American people two entire generations.

The distinguished Edward Everett, delivered a lecture in Salem, Mass., June, 1833, fifty-five years ago, in which, among other things, he said: The maxims of temperance are not new; they are as old as Christianity; as old as any of the inculations of personal and social duty. Every other instrument of moral censure had been tried, in the case of intemperance, as in that of other prevailing vices, crimes, and errors. The law had done something; the press had done something; the stated ministration of religion had done something, but altogether had done but little; and intemperance had reached a most alarming degree of prevalence. At length, the principle of association was applied; societies were formed, meetings were held, public addresses made, information collected and com-

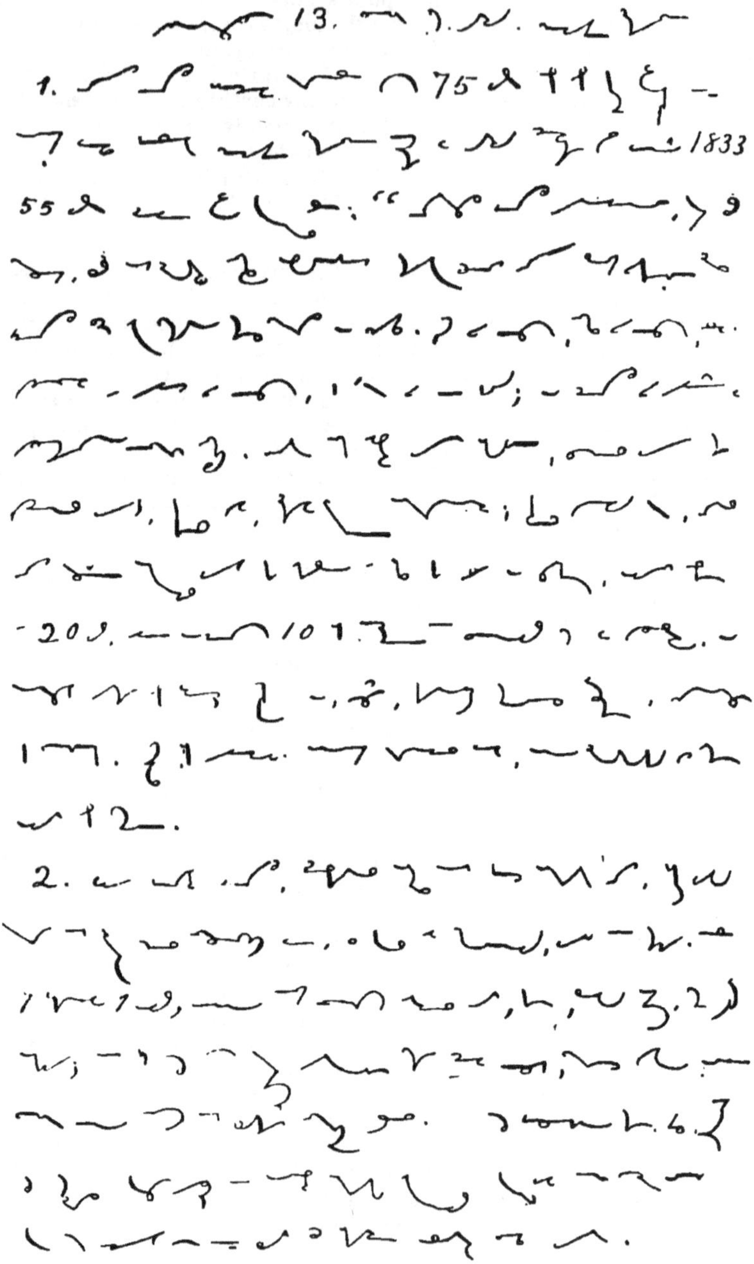

municated, pledges mutually given, the minds of men excited, and their hearts warmed, by comparison of opinions, by concert and sympathy; and within the space of twenty years, of which not more than ten have been devoted to strenuous effort, a most signal and unexampled reform has been achieved. The bubbling, and, as it seemed perennial fountains of this vice have, in many cases, been dried up. Villages have been regenerated, and entire communities changed, and an incalculable amount of vice and woe has been prevented.

2. When we contemplate intemperance, in all its bearings and effects on the condition and character of men, I believe we shall come to the conclusion, that it is the greatest evil, which, as beings of a compound nature, we have to fear. It is the arch-abomination of our natures; tending to assure the triumph of that which is low, base, sensual and earthly, over the heavenly and pure; to convert this so curiously organized frame into a disordered, crazy machine, and to drag down the soul to the slavery of groveling lusts.

This all-destroying vice ruins the health of its victims. They seem resolved to anticipate the corruption of their natures. They cannot wait to get sick and die. They think the worm is too slow in his approach, and sluggish at his work.

It is a double death, by which they drag about with them above the grave a mass of diseased, decaying aching flesh. They will not only commit suicide, but do it in such a way as to be the witnesses, and concious victims of the cruel process of self murder; doing it by degrees, quenching the sight, benumbing the brain, and changing a fair, healthy, robust frame into a shrinking, suffering living corpse, with nothing of vitality but the power of suffering, and with everything of death but its peace.

3. Then follows the wreck of property; ruin, which comes like an avenging angel to waste the substance of the intemperate; which crosses their threshold, commissioned as it were, to plague them with all the horrors of ruined fortune and blasted prospects; and passes before their astonished sight, in the dread array of affairs perplexed, debts accumulated, substance squandered, honor tainted, wife and children cast out upon the mercy of the world.

4. Bad as all this is, much as it is, it is neither the greatest nor the worst part of the aggravations of the crime of intemperance. It produces consequences of still more awful moment. It first exasperates the passions, and then takes off from them the restraints of the reason and the will; maddens and then unchains the tiger, ravening for blood; tramples all the intellectual and moral man under the feet of the stimulated clay; lays the understanding, the kind affections, and the conscience in the same grave with prosperity and health; and having killed the body, kills the soul!

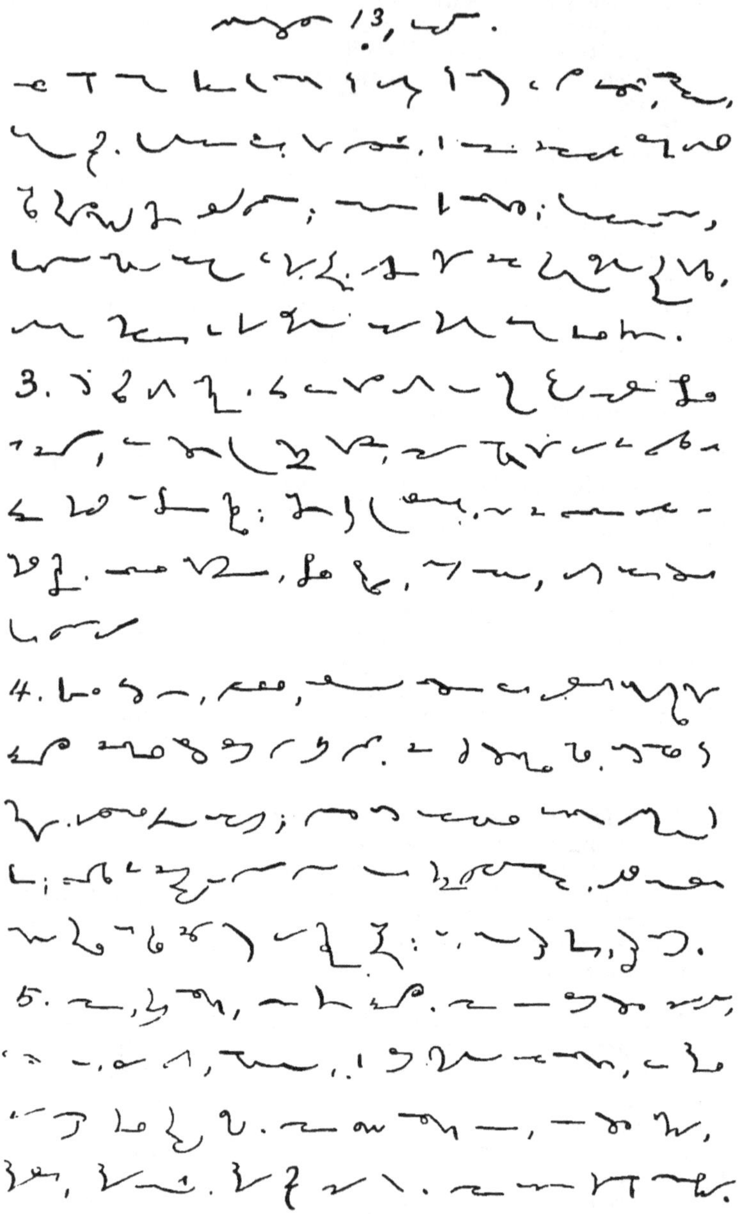
13,
3.
4.
5.

5. Such, faintly described, is the vice of imtemperance. Such it still exists in our land; checked, and, as we hope, declining, but still prevailing to a degree which invites all our zeal for its effectual suppression. Such as I have described it, it exists, I fear, in every city, in every town, in every village in our country. Such and so formidable is its power.

700 words to be written in 7 minutes and reduced to 5 minutes.

www.ingramcontent.com/pod-product-compliance
Lightning Source LLC
Chambersburg PA
CBHW032242080426
42735CB00008B/965